J.S. MILL

A BEGINNER'S GUIDE

J.S. MILL

A BEGINNER'S GUIDE

MICHEL PETHERAM

Series Editors
Rob Abbott & Charlie Bell

Hodder & Stoughton
A MEMBER OF THE HODDER HEADLINE GROUP

Acknowledgements

To my father, who also introduced me to books and ideas, but much more gently than John Stuart Mill's father did.

Orders: please contact Bookpoint Ltd, 130 Milton Park, Abingdon, Oxon OX14 4SB. Telephone: (44) 01235 827720, Fax: (44) 01235 400554. Lines are open from 9.00–6.00, Monday to Saturday, with a 24-hour message answering service. Email address: orders@bookpoint.co.uk

British Library Cataloguing in Publication Data
A catalogue record for this title is available from The British Library

ISBN 0 340 80474 2

First published 2002
Impression number   10 9 8 7 6 5 4 3 2 1
Year 2007 2006 2005 2004 2003 2002

Cover photo from Hulton-Deutsch Collection/Corbis.
Typeset by Transet Limited, Coventry, England.
Printed in Great Britain for Hodder & Stoughton Educational, a division of Hodder Headline Plc, 338 Euston Road, London NW1 3BH by Cox & Wyman, Reading, Berks.

CONTENTS

Preface

John Stuart Mill was the greatest British philosopher of the nineteenth century and, at the same time, very much a public thinker. He was moved to think by what he saw of the world around him. He wanted to promote the improvement of human society in everything he wrote. One of the main reasons why his major works are important is because they were prompted by issues that still concern us today, over 100 years later. He was also a public thinker in the sense that he was not a university teacher, but had a career as a senior civil servant, while writing in his spare time; he was also an MP for three years. This book aims to give an understanding of Mill's most important ideas and to show how they still affect philosophical debate today.

J.S. Mill – A Beginner's Guide is organised into 11 chapters and each chapter ends with a summary. The first two chapters describe Mill's active life. The remainder of the book concentrates, as Mill would have wanted, on his writings. Chapters 3 and 4 look at his utilitarianism and Chapters 5, 6 and 7 discuss important aspects of his famous long essay *On Liberty*. Chapter 8 describes Mill's radical feminist ideas and Chapter 9, his political ideas. These are followed by a short chapter on the extent and variety of Mill's other writings. The book ends with a brief assessment of Mill's qualities as a thinker.

If you ever question what happiness is, what people should be free to do and what exactly democracy is, this book is a good place to start to find the answers.

The prodigy

John Stuart Mill was once asked for a summary of his life by an American journalist. He replied simply: 'my life contains no incidents which in any way concern the public; and with the exception of my writings, which are open to everyone, there are no materials for such a biographical sketch as you contemplate. The only matter which I can furnish is a few dates.'

This self-effacement is typical of Mill, as is the emphasis on his writings – and it is with his works that this account shall be mostly concerned. But matters are not quite so simple and it was Mill who complicated them. By writing an autobiography and allowing it to be published after his death, Mill himself turned the spotlight on his own life and in particular on his remarkable and now notorious education.

MILL'S EDUCATION

John Stuart Mill was born in London on 20 May 1806. Britain was at war with France, where Napoleon had been in power since 1799. In 1805 Britain had, by winning the Battle of Trafalgar, gained command of the seas of the world. This naval domination would give Britain the opportunity to increase its empire and become the most powerful nation in the world by the end of the nineteenth century. However, this was also a period when radical ideas had been stimulated by the French Revolution and there was much political debate in Britain, in which Mill's father joined.

Mill's father, James Mill, had been born into a poor Scottish family but he had managed to go to the University of Edinburgh, which at the time was one of the liveliest educational institutions in Britain. Then, like so many Scotsmen before and since, he came to London to make his fortune. He married, started a family and obtained a post with the

East India Company, which at that time governed India, one of the prized possessions of Britain's Empire.

The turning point in James Mill's life was meeting the utilitarian thinker, Jeremy Bentham (1748–1832). Bentham had a deep influence on James Mill and this influence would be passed on to the next generation. Their utilitarian ideas will be explained in Chapter 3.

James Mill was much admired for his sharp intellect and wide knowledge. John Stuart Mill wrote of 'that force and decision which characterised all that came from him'. On the other hand, he had scarcely any belief in pleasure or enjoyment. James Mill would encourage in his son a devotion to the 'improvement of mankind', hard intellectual work, selfless dedication and great energy in tackling the forces of unreason and tradition.

One of the reasons John Stuart Mill gave for writing his autobiography was to give a record of 'an education which was unusual and remarkable'. Mill did not go to school. His father started him on Greek from the age of three. This was shortly followed by arithmetic. At the age of seven he began Latin and reading **Homer** in the original. Before his tenth birthday he had gone on to **Plato's** dialogues. In fact, the story of Mill's childhood is mostly the story of his reading, in the main directed by his father. There was time for 'lighter' reading, which for Mill was history, in particular Greek and Roman history. But his favourite book was *Robinson Crusoe*.

KEY FACT

Homer (8th century BC): Greek epic poet, author of the *Iliad* and the *Odyssey*, the earliest poems of Western civilization.

Plato (c.429–347 BC): the great Greek philosopher who had immense influence on all Western philosophy. His writings consist of some 30 dialogues, all of which have survived.

All of this sounds like extremely hard work. The common reaction has been one of astonishment and sometimes horror. However, Mill was careful to point out that this was not an education of 'cram', as he put it. He was not forcibly stuffed with facts. In following the long list of difficult and demanding books that the young Mill read, it is easy to miss an important feature of James Mill's teaching method. The younger Mill would go on walks with his father, daily before breakfast, and would have to give an account of what he had read the day before. This exercise would have encouraged Mill's attention to his reading, tested his understanding and his own powers of summarizing and explaining in his own words. To have done this from such an early age did much to develop the sharpness of Mill's mind. This was one-to-one teaching, which is the most effective pupil–teacher ratio. In addition, this teaching was not geared to passing tests and exams, but entirely to ensuring the student's understanding. For Mill it was an education in thinking for himself.

Nor were Mill's achievements unique. William Pitt the Younger who had died in the year of Mill's birth, became Prime Minister at the age of 23 and could read Latin and Greek at the age of ten. Bentham himself went to Oxford at the age of 12. It is likely that Mill's father thought his son could emulate these examples. That Mill did so much Greek and Latin is not unusual. All education at the time was based on the classics and there was hardly any literature for children. Another remarkable fact for the time is that Mill was brought up without any religious belief.

It was something of an educational experiment. But to be conducted properly, Mill had to be undistracted by school or the company of other children. This meant that Mill's was an isolated childhood. The rewards for his early ability were to be given the tasks of teaching his younger brothers and sisters (he was the eldest of nine children) and of helping to correct the proofs of his father's *History of British India*, published in 1817, when Mill was 11. Another disadvantage was James

Mill's stern, even irritable character. He was unable to show affection to his children.

It is no surprise that Mill once commented 'I never was a boy'. On the other hand, Mill claimed that he had a happy childhood and took pleasure in his learning. As an education it was clearly successful; it was far better than the one he would have had at university. Mill reckoned that he had been given a 25-year start on his contemporaries.

THE DEVELOPMENT OF A PHILOSOPHER

Mill's education was a many-sided one. There was his aptitude for languages and history. At the age of 13 he was introduced by his father to economics, a subject that would interest him for the rest of his life. Moreover, politics would have been discussed regularly in the household.

But, his main reputation now is as a philosopher. From the age of 12 Mill embarked on logic – no easy textbooks, but the difficult works of **Aristotle**. The young Mill clearly had a talent for this subject. There is much more to philosophy than logic, but Mill's claim that 'the first intellectual operation in which I arrived at any proficiency, was dissecting a bad argument' is justified by the sharpness of mind that is seen in all of his writing. This ability was supplemented by reading more Plato, one of his father's favourite authors, and acquiring a familiarity with the Socratic method, that is, **Socrates'** practice of finding truth through cross-examination, which, said Mill, 'as an education for precise thinking, is inestimable'.

KEY FACT

Aristotle (384–322 BC): pupil of Plato, a scientist as well as philosopher and the first to write works on logic.

Socrates (469–399 BC): Greek philosopher, who wrote nothing. However, thanks to Plato's portrait of him, he is one of the most living personalities in Western culture, not least because he was executed for his beliefs.

It has already been mentioned that Mill's father became friendly with Bentham. This was an enlargement of Mill's own life too. He would join Bentham and his father for long stays in the country, for Bentham spent half of each year in Somerset. Then Bentham's brother, General Sir Samuel Bentham, invited Mill to accompany his family to France in 1820, when Mill was 14. Mill learnt French and attended university lectures on science in that language, which is more evidence of his precocity. 'But', he wrote, 'the greatest, perhaps, of the many advantages which I owed to this episode in my education, was that of having breathed for a whole year the free and genial atmosphere of Continental life'. In other words, it was a refreshing contrast from Britain. Mill may also have enjoyed the freedom of being away from his severe father.

What he found in France was that people expressed their feelings freely, something the nineteenth-century English did not do. It is interesting that his criticism of the English in this part of the *Autobiography* points to the same disdain for feeling he noted in his father. One of the problems he was to grapple with was what role in life to give to the emotions. Another benefit he drew from his visit abroad was that he was able, through his knowledge of French, to become familiar with continental thought on political questions which he thought, preserved him from the 'parochialism' of the English.

On his return from France, Mill continued to study with his father. He took classes in law and a career as a barrister was considered for him. But now there occurred 'one of the turning points in my mental history'. Mill was, of course, very familiar with Bentham's utilitarian ideas, but he now read his works closely for the first time.

He responded to Bentham's precise critical method, 'his intellectual clearness', and the possibility of making practical improvements in human affairs. Mill felt that he had now achieved a much deeper understanding of the principle of 'utility'.

'It gave unity to my conceptions of things. I now had opinions; a creed, a doctrine, a philosophy; in one among the best senses of the word, a religion; the inculcation and diffusion of which could be made the principal outward purpose of a life. And I had a grand conception laid before me of changes to be effected in the condition of mankind through that doctrine.' From this time forth, Mill had 'an object in life: to be a reformer of the world'.

Mill read more of Bentham's works and also the philosophers **Locke** and **Helvetius**. In the summer of 1822, aged 16, he wrote his first argumentative essay, an attack on aristocratic prejudices. There is also a story that, about this time, he was arrested for handing out pamphlets on birth control to the London poor – the charge was one of distributing obscene literature. Meanwhile, a group of young men had gathered around his father, who had become a very influential figure in the radical movement for reform of government towards greater democracy. Mill joined their discussions and was accepted as an equal. In the same year he formed a discussion group called the Utilitarian Society and enjoyed his first publications, which were letters to newspapers. Mill called this period one of 'youthful propagandism'.

KEY FACT

John Locke (1632–1704: English philosopher, famous as the senior figure of British empiricism, a school that links knowledge to experience.

Claude-Adrien Helvetius (1715–1771): French philosopher. An empiricist like Locke and also an important influence on Bentham.

In May 1823, Mill joined the East India Company where James Mill was continuing his successful career. This meant, however, that Mill was still working closely with his father. Besides this regular employment, Mill became, from early 1825, a sort of editorial assistant to Bentham, to help him prepare his works for publication. This was not an easy task; Mill had to condense and construct the books from Bentham's disorganized masses of papers.

At the age of 20, then, all seemed to be going well for Mill. He had a secure and interesting job. He was active in his leisure time and a frequent contributor to the press. And he was part of a lively group of young men, embarked on a larger cause.

MILL'S CRISIS

Nevertheless, in the autumn of 1826, a few months after his twentieth birthday, Mill suffered what he called 'a crisis in my mental history'. One day he had asked himself: '"Suppose that all your objects in life were realized; that all the changes in institutions and opinions which you are looking forward to, could be completely effected at this very instant: would this be a great joy and happiness to you?" And an irrepressible self-consciousness distinctly answered, "No!" At this my heart sank within me: the whole foundation on which my life was constructed fell down ... I seemed to have nothing left to live for.' Mill felt that his ability at analysis had completely worn away his feelings. Nothing gave him pleasure. He had no one to share this crisis with, least of all his father. It was a crisis, but not a breakdown, for he was able to go on mechanically with his usual occupations. He fell into a state of depression that deepened and stayed with him for several months. And he began to think of suicide.

The beginning of his recovery is vividly told: 'I was reading, accidentally, Marmontel's Memoirs, and came to the passage which relates his father's death, the distressed position of the family, and the sudden inspiration by which he, then a mere boy, felt and made them feel that he would be everything to them – would supply the place of all that had been lost. A vivid conception of the scene and its feelings came over me, and I was moved to tears. From this moment, my burthen grew lighter. The oppression of the thought that all feeling was dead within me, was gone. I was no longer hopeless: I was not a stock or a stone. I had still, it seemed, some of the material out of which all worth of character, and all capacity for happiness, are made.'

There has been much discussion of this crisis. Some have picked up on the mention of the father's death in the reading of Marmontel and argued that Mill had suppressed his feelings of aggression towards his father. It has been claimed that he was suffering from frustrated ambition, that he would have liked to go into politics, a career move that was no longer possible now that he was working for the East India Company. Others have argued that it was caused by overwork – this would certainly have been a contributory factor, for demands had been and were being made on him from all sides. Another factor is a philosophical one. Mill had come, as he suggests, to see the inadequacy of the utilitarianism of Bentham and his father.

Whatever the reason or mixture of reasons for the crisis, Mill shows his strength of character in his willingness to learn from the experience. He drew two conclusions.

First, although he still believed that happiness was the purpose of life, he now thought it could only be attained indirectly. 'Ask yourself whether you are happy, and you cease to be so. The only chance is to treat, not happiness, but some end external to it, as the purpose of life.'

Second, for the first time, Mill gave an important place, as part of human happiness, to 'the internal culture of the individual'. He did not deny any of what he had believed before about the importance of the development of the intellectual faculties, the skills of analysis and rationality. However, this had to be balanced, with the help of the arts, like poetry and painting. 'The cultivation of the feelings became one of the cardinal points in my ethical and philosophical creed.'

✻ ✻ ✻ SUMMARY ✻ ✻ ✻

● John Stuart Mill was born in London in 1806.

● His father, James Mill, was a strong personality and was influenced by Jeremy Bentham.

● His father began Mill's education at the age of three, by starting to teach him Greek.

● Mill's remarkable education, directed by his father, gave him a very effective intellectual training.

● At the age of 20, Mill suffered a 'mental crisis' for which many reasons have been given. The important thing is that Mill recovered and gained, he thought, a greater understanding of human happiness.

2 Public life

The years that followed Mill's crisis and period of depression were years of gradual recovery, both in his personal life and in his work. The first step towards his restoration was the discovery of the poetry of **Wordsworth**, which occurred in the autumn of 1828. In it he found

his own love of natural scenery, not just description, but deep feelings aroused by that scenery. Wordsworth's poetry confirmed to Mill that his education had neglected the emotions. He found in it 'a source of inward joy, of sympathetic and imaginative pleasure'. In turning to poetry, he went on to read many more of the **Romantic** writers, such as Shelley, Goethe and Coleridge. Later he reviewed books of poems by Tennyson and Browning.

KEY FACT

William Wordsworth 1770–1850): English poet, one of the first British Romatic writers and a supreme poet of nature.

This in turn suggests a generation gap, though one rather different from those between modern parents and teenagers. Mill's father, like many of his generation, had valued the development of the intellectual faculties. It was reason alone that man needed. The Romantics found this a one-sided and narrow approach, and called for the development of the whole human being. Ideas like these were the antidote he needed to Bentham and James Mill. Therefore, as well as being a step in his recovery, the discovery of poetry was a step in his emancipation from his father's influence. An even greater one began in 1830.

HARRIET TAYLOR

During the summer of 1830, Mill was invited to a dinner party at the house of a John Taylor, a successful businessman in the city. He had a young wife, Harriet, who had ambitions as a writer and who was just a year younger than Mill. Their friendship gradually deepened. Mill became a frequent visitor to the Taylor's home and then Harriet was writing to Mill as 'the only being who has ever called forth all my feelings.' They were in love with each other.

Harriet and her husband had a trial separation, but a situation like this was a very difficult one in this period. Divorce was not a real possibility, for it could only be obtained on the grounds of adultery or brutality. Harriet had three small children and remained fond of her husband. Divorce would also have badly damaged Mill's career. After a fair amount of emotional toing and froing, Mill and Harriet settled into a relationship of close companionship, spending weekends and holidays together. This state of affairs was tolerated by her husband, for he and Harriet were mostly living apart. It lasted many years, but there is no evidence and little likelihood that Mill and Harriet became lovers. In 1849 John Taylor died and Mill married Harriet at last in 1851.

Mill called her 'the most admirable person I had ever known', and described her as 'a woman of deep and strong feeling, of penetrating and intuitive intelligence, of an eminently meditative and poetic nature.' It would seem that in her he found that sensitivity to feeling which he had missed in his upbringing and which he had come to realize was what he needed. She seems to have taken over his father's role as guide and stimulator. He also said that she made a large contribution to much of his writing. To Mill she was a complete, fully-rounded person. He also felt that her abilities had been stifled, 'shut out by the social disabilities of women from any adequate exercise of her higher faculties in action on the world without.' In his autobiography, Mill praises her even more than this. In fact, he over-praises her to the point that readers have rebelled, for no one could be so perfect.

MILL THE WRITER

In the years after he met Harriet, from his mid-twenties onwards, Mill continued to work at the East India Company's offices in the City of London. Mill worked in the Examiner's Office, alongside his father, until the latter's death in 1836. This department was responsible for drafting letters, instructions and other communications to the administration in India. Mill was, in effect, a civil servant.

One thing this work gave him was experience of practical affairs and of the compromises often required to get things done. It also gave him security and the time to write. Mill was required to attend the office for six hours a day, but was able to do the work of the company in rather less. The rest of the time he could spend on his writing or in meeting friends who called on him. This must have been acceptable to his superiors for Mill was promoted regularly.

Thus, Mill was able to maintain a career as a journalist in parallel to one as a civil servant. He was a journalist in the old-fashioned sense of the word, one who contributed to journals, not a reporter. His first publications were mainly essays and book reviews. The journals of the nineteenth century were serious, usually solemn, publications. They assumed a long attention span in their readers. This allowed writers to develop their ideas and arguments at length.

Mill wrote mostly for **liberal** and **radical** journals. One was the *Westminster Review*, which was funded by Bentham. Mill contributed on a wide range of topics: Ireland, the French Revolution, economics, currency issues, ancient Greek history, psychology, land tenure, reform of the House of Lords and, of course, philosophy. Although his output was so varied, his main interest was in campaigning for political reform.

KEYWORDS

Liberal: another word difficult to define. Political liberalism in the nineteenth century was in a favour of free trade, and political reform, leading to democracy.

Radical: favouring thorough social and political reform.

At this point it is necessary to say something about parliamentary reform in Britain at this time. At the beginning of the nineteenth century the system of parliamentary representation was full of anomalies. Migration of the population to new industrial regions had created urban areas that had no members of parliament at all, while some old constituencies had only a handful of voters. These were known as 'Rotten Boroughs'. There were still 'Pocket Boroughs' where powerful men in the area could more or less nominate who they wanted. There was no uniform basis for who could vote and who could not. The first Reform Act, in 1832, abolished rotten and pocket boroughs. There was a redistribution of seats and the vote was extended – but to the upper middle classes only.

Mill was part of a radical group who hoped to keep up the momentum of reform after this first act. But they found that most politicians thought they had done enough and that the public showed little interest. After years of campaigning and writing, Mill began to despair of political success and started working more systematically on philosophy. In 1843, he published A *System of Logic*, which had taken 13 years to write. After a short breather he began another large work in 1845, the *Principles of Political Economy*, which was published in 1848. Both were surprisingly successful. These works are little read now but they quickly established his nineteenth-century reputation, for they became standard textbooks in their subjects for decades.

RETIREMENT

Having waited so long for their marriage, Mill and Harriet were unable to enjoy it fully. Mill suffered from tuberculosis. His father had died of it and so would two of his brothers. A year after their marriage, Harriet had caught it. By 1854 they both expected to die within a year. To recover, Mill took a six-month break in the warmer climates of Italy and Greece. This travel cure worked, and in 1856 Mill was promoted to the post of Chief Examiner (a post his father had held) at the East India Company, having served there for over 33 years. But just two years later, as a result of the Indian Mutiny of 1857, the Company was wound up and the administration of India was taken over by the British government. Mill was able to retire.

Mill was now free and at the end of the year he and Harriet took a holiday in southern France. However, her tuberculosis suddenly returned and she died in Avignon, where she was buried.

The fundamental vigour of Mill's mind is shown by the work he did after her death, when other men might have lapsed into silent grief. What is more, these are the works for which he is most remembered. He published *On Liberty* in 1859, immediately after Harriet's death. It was a work on which they had worked closely together in the last two years. He regarded it as her memorial. In 1860 and 1861 he wrote *Considerations on Representative Government* and *The Subjection of Women* (which was not published until 1869). *Utilitarianism* followed in 1863.

The Subjection of Women was written at the suggestion of Helen Taylor, Harriet's daughter. She had been very close to her mother. She now gave her affection to Mill and was his close companion for the last 14 years of his life. After his death, she prepared for publication his posthumous works, including his *Autobiography*.

BACK TO POLITICS

Mill had recovered his place as a leading light in liberal circles. Once more in the public eye, he shortly became a unique figure, a philosopher in parliament.

In March 1865 he received a letter asking if he would be willing to stand for the constituency of Westminster in the forthcoming general election. Westminster was then a liberal and radical stronghold. He hesitated at first and then set out some very unusual terms. He would not support any local interests. He would promote the views he had expressed in his writings but otherwise would vote independently and not according to party loyalty. He would not canvas for his election. Lastly, he would not contribute to the cost of his election.

One contemporary commented that God himself would not be elected if he made those conditions. Much to his surprise Mill was chosen as a candidate. This had the benefit of causing a boom in sales of his books and widespread discussion of his ideas. Even more to his surprise Mill was elected in July 1865, defeating the Conservative candidate, W.H. Smith (the son in W. H. Smith and Son).

Mill first entered the House of Commons in February 1866, with a Liberal government. Gladstone was the leading figure in the Commons and Lord John Russell (grandfather of Bertrand Russell) was Prime Minister. His first speeches in the Commons were poor but, always a quick learner, he was able to profit from his mistakes and went on to make impressive and respected contributions to debates. He supported the Liberal government until its fall, only a few months later, in June. The Conservatives took over. This gave Mill more freedom. He had not gone into parliament with the hope of a political career, but because it would give him the opportunity to raise issues that he thought were important. Now that he no longer had to support the government, he could advocate his radical views. Not that he was extreme. He had learnt from his years with the East India Company something of the negotiations and concessions required in public action. He was, as one writer has remarked, 'a shrewd idealist'.

The great parliamentary issue of the day was a new Reform Act. This one would give the vote to 1 million town labourers. The debates in the Commons gave Mill the opportunity to raise the issue of women's suffrage, the first time the topic was raised there, a fact that made Mill very proud. During the debates on reform, he proposed that the word 'man' be replaced by 'person'. He did not expect to win the vote, but his great success was to have the subject taken seriously, when it could so easily have been ridiculed. His proposal received very fair coverage in the newspapers and even some support in editorials. And Mill was delighted to have 73 votes on his side.

Mill spoke for the minority view on two other subjects, again showing himself to be ahead of his time. He criticised the policy of British governments towards Ireland and spoke in favour of taking a more lenient and sympathetic approach, at a time when there had been cases of terrorism. The other case involved Governor Eyre of Jamaica who had put down a revolt in that British colony with extreme brutality and considerable illegality. Eyre was dismissed, but for Mill this was not enough. He thought that the governor should be tried for murder. Most of the British public, however, supported Eyre; Mill received abusive letters and even threats of assassination.

LAST YEARS

A general election was called in 1868, with a newly enlarged electorate. It was a convincing win for the Liberal party, but Mill was defeated. He believed this was for a combination of reasons. He claimed that the Tory party was able to spend a lot more money than the Liberals on the election in his constituency. He had lost personal popularity with many sectors of political opinion for his attacks on Eyre and also for his public support of an outspoken atheist, Charles Bradlaugh. Mill suggested that he had been too independent for many of his liberal supporters.

Yet Mill was relieved, 'so great and fresh is the pleasure of freedom, and the return to the only occupations which agree with my tastes and habits.' He was so relieved that he turned down invitations to stand as member of parliament for other constituencies. He returned to his writing and spent much of his time in Avignon, in the house he had bought near the graveyard where Harriet was buried.

His main work was done, but he finished *Three Essays on Religion* and brought the *Autobiography* up to date. He produced new editions of the *Principles of Political Economy* and *A System of Logic*, which shows their continuing success. His time as an MP had turned him into a national figure. Instead of the television appearances that this might mean now, he received hundreds of letters, to most of which he replied. He had not lost interest in politics. He began a book on socialism and he kept up with the suffragette movement.

Mill had loved the outdoors from his youth and since his admiration for Wordsworth. In France he became friendly with Fabre, who would become famous as an entomologist. They shared an interest in botany and would often go on walks together. In 1873, on another walking holiday in the Vaucluse in France, Mill contracted erysipelas (a fever with inflammation of the skin) and died within three days. His final words to Helen Taylor were 'You know I have done my work'. He was buried in Avignon beside Harriet.

✳ ✳ ✳ SUMMARY ✳ ✳ ✳

- Mill broadened his outlook, first, through poetry, and then through his relationship with Harriet Taylor whom he met in 1830 and married in 1851.

- While working for the East India Company, he was a frequent contributor to Victorian journals.

- When his hopes for political reform faded, he turned to writing philosophical works.

- Shortly after his retirement, Harriet died. Mill then wrote and published his best-known philosophical works.

- He served a few years as an MP and became an important public figure.

- He died in 1873 in France.

3 The utilitarian

The main intellectual influence on Mill was the utilitarianism of his father and Jeremy Bentham. Bentham did not claim to be an originator of the ideas. He claimed that they went back to the ancient Greeks. Nevertheless it was he who established utilitarianism as an important school of thought in the nineteenth century. It is familiar even to those who have no interest in philosophy. Whenever we try to decide what to do by counting up in some way the possible benefits of a course of action, we are engaged in a kind of utilitarian reasoning.

BENTHAM'S UTILITARIANISM

The word 'utilitarianism' is derived from 'utility' and is a rather odd word in the context of moral philosophy. However, it is simply an old-fashioned way of saying 'usefulness'. Bentham looked for the usefulness or, as we would now say, the consequences of an action. There are two crucial points. First, we should judge the rightness or wrongness of actions by their consequences. Second, these consequences should be measured by the happiness the action caused. So Bentham's 'principle of utility' is, as he puts it in his legalistic language, a principle which 'approves or disapproves of every action whatsoever, according to the tendency which it appears to have to augment or diminish the happiness of the party whose interest is in question.' An action is right if it promotes happiness, wrong if it opposes happiness.

For a time Bentham used the catch-phrase 'the greatest happiness of the greatest number', but he developed doubts about this because it appeared to mean that the happiness of the majority was all that mattered. The trouble with phrasing it in this way is that it implied that it would be all right to harshly oppress a minority for a small gain in the happiness of the majority, with the result that the overall amount of happiness was reduced. Later in his life Bentham preferred to use the label 'the greatest happiness principle' which has the implication that he wanted; that we should aim for the greatest happiness overall, however this is shared out.

And how is happiness to be measured? According to Bentham, by how far it produces pleasure and prevents pain. This is the third crucial point in Bentham's utilitarianism. He thought that any particular pleasure or pain has a value that can be assessed or calculated and which can then be compared against other pleasures and pains. So, when an individual or a government is faced by a choice between two courses of action, they should add up the benefits of each (measure in amounts of pleasure or pain) and choose the one which will cause the most pleasure or the least pain. Bentham describes in some detail how pleasures and pains can be measured. The two main measurable characteristics of a pleasure are how long it lasts and how intense it is. So the pleasure of lingering over half a bottle of wine is greater than quickly swallowing one glass; and the 'intensity' of the pleasure will be greater if it is a vintage wine instead of an ordinary table wine.

To sum up Bentham's argument: the rightness of an action depends on its utility, that is, its consequences in increasing or decreasing happiness. Increases and decreases in happiness are to be measured in amounts of pleasure and pain.

To illustrate this with an issue that is still the subject of hot debate, take capital punishment. A utilitarian does not believe that the death penalty should be inflicted for murder on the grounds of retribution, simply to punish. He or she will consider the *consequences* of capital punishment. The main issues will be whether this punishment acts as a deterrent to would-be murderers and whether it is more or less cruel than life imprisonment. Another harmful consequence of capital punishment is the likelihood that sooner or later an innocent person will be executed.

In the early nineteenth century, Bentham's 'greatest happiness principle' was a very radical way of looking at morality. Most people then believed that the Bible, as the word of God, told us what to do. We just had to follow God's commands, as explained by Christianity. Even now many people believe that a morality has to be based on religious commands and supported by promises of heaven. Utilitarianism, however, is firmly non-religious. It puts its emphasis on people's happiness, here in this world.

Utilitarianism was politically radical too. For Bentham the happiness of a society consisted in the happiness of the individuals within it. To govern 'in the public interest' is to govern in line with what most people in that society prefer. So governments should he subject to control by most of the people. In other words, they should be democratic.

It was also radical in the way that it required justifications for courses of action. It would be no good to rely on tradition 'this is the way we have always done it' or even to say 'this is what my conscience tells me to do'. Bentham asks 'what are the benefits?' As Mill said 'To Bentham more than any other source might be traced the questing spirit, the disposition to demand the why of everything'; this made him 'the great subversive' of the age.

MILL'S UTILITARIANISM

Mill's famous essay, *Utilitarianism,* was first published in 1861 as a series of magazine articles and in 1863 as a book. It is quite short, about 70 pages in modern editions. It is also clear and eloquent. It has become one of the classic works in moral philosophy. Because it was aimed at a general audience it is not difficult to read. At the same time, it deals with complicated and important issues.

It is the culmination of Mill's debate with utilitarianism since his youth. He had taken it up with enthusiasm, then, after his mental crisis, come close to rejecting it entirely. In the 1830s he had written essays that were strongly critical of Bentham. But he swung back, perhaps as a result of Harriet's influence which caused Mill to recover some of his early radicalism. He certainly shared Bentham's attachment to democracy and his rejection of tradition.

In fact, Mill begins his book with a statement of the principle which sounds very much like Bentham himself: 'The creed which accepts as the foundation of morals, Utility, or the Greatest Happiness Principle, holds that actions are right in proportion as they tend to promote happiness, wrong as they tend to produce the reverse of happiness. By happiness is intended pleasure, and the absence of pain; by unhappiness, pain and the privation of pleasure.'

The emphasis on pleasure, begun by Bentham and now repeated by Mill, had led many critics of utilitarianism to complain that it was a 'pig philosophy', because it suggested that all there was to life was, as an old phrase puts it, 'wine, women and song' or, in the newer one, 'sex, drugs and rock and roll.' This is not really fair to Bentham, who thought that any experience that gives a person pleasure should be valued. Reading a book on philosophy can count as much as drinking champagne. But Bentham did also say that 'prejudice apart, the game of push-pin is of equal value with the arts and sciences of music and poetry' (push-pin was a very simple children's game). This notion of 'push-pin as good as poetry' evidently made a strong and unpleasant impression on Mill, because poetry had become very important to him. It seemed to sum up the narrowness of Bentham's conception of happiness.

Mill thought that he could counter this criticism of 'pig philosophy'. He argued that the greatest happiness principle was broader than Bentham (and his own father) had recognised and could incorporate what human beings valued beyond simple pleasure.

His first step was to argue that 'some *kinds* of pleasure are more desirable and valuable than others.' Bentham had been content to calculate the *quantity* of pleasures; Mill claimed that we also have to consider their *quality*. Given two different pleasures, if one of them is preferred by all or by most of those who have experienced both, then that is the more desirable pleasure. If it is valued so highly that no one would give it up for any quantity of the other pleasure, then we can conclude that this pleasure is superior in quality. Mill adds that, as a matter of fact, people who are familiar with the full range of human pleasures, in the widest sense, prefer lives which employ their 'higher faculties'.

Imagine an oyster granted eternal life. Every day until infinity it has the pleasure of basking in warm water, a pleasure similar to the one human beings enjoy when soaking in a warm bath. Compare this to the life of a typical human being, which includes disappointments, struggles, illness and eventual death. Whatever the pleasures experienced in that human life, the pleasure of eternally being an oyster must eventually be greater. So on Bentham's type of calculation, this would be the life to be preferred. But most, if not all of us, would reject this and Mill, with his notion of quality in pleasures, suggests why we would. Human beings have distinctive capacities and will not be fully satisfied by a life which does not involve exercising them. 'It is better to be a human being dissatisfied than a pig satisfied; better to be Socrates dissatisfied than a fool satisfied' as Mill famously wrote. The pig or the fool might disagree, but this is because they only know their own kind of pleasure, that is, of being a pig or a fool.

This may seem rather elitist. However, Mill is not saying that everyone should give up the 'lower' pleasures for the 'higher' ones. It is because we have higher faculties that we will not be fully satisfied by a life that does not use them.

Another line of attack on the narrowness of Bentham's utilitarianism was to say that happiness is not the only thing that matters. Many people have actually given up their own happiness for the sake of others and are rightly admired for their self-sacrifice. In reply to this Mill agrees that those heroes and martyrs have gone without their own happiness for a higher goal. But what is that goal? Surely, says Mill, it is the happiness of others. Would we value anyone's self-sacrifice if it did not produce any benefits for his or her fellow human beings, in other words, if it had no good consequences?

At this point Mill makes a strong statement: 'The happiness which forms the utilitarian standard of what is right in conduct, is not the agent's own happiness but that of all concerned. As between his own happiness and that of theirs, utilitarianism requires him to be

> **KEYWORD**
>
> Altruistic: disinterested concern for the welfare of others.

as strictly impartial as a disinterested and benevolent spectator.' Here we see Mill give utilitarianism a firmly **altruistic** slant.

There is another way of arguing, against Bentham, that the pursuit of happiness is not everything. Apart from the people who appear to sacrifice their own happiness, there are those who pursue other aims than happiness. These other aims are pursued for their own sake, such as virtue or music or health. There are also less admirable aims, such as money, power or fame. How does Mill deal with these?

'The ingredients of happiness are very various' he admits, but anything that is desired for its own sake is desired by people 'as a part of their happiness ... they are included in happiness. They are some of the elements of which the desire of happiness is made up'.

In attempting to incorporate these other 'ingredients' into an overall conception of happiness, Mill has moved a long way from Bentham's calculations of amounts of pleasure. Perhaps he has moved too far.

THE ATTRACTIONS OF UTILITARIANISM

There are problems in Mill's arguments, which shall be considered in the next chapter. Nevertheless, the strongest critics of utilitarianism have admitted that it is plausible and even attractive. It still has energetic supporters after nearly 200 years.

First of all, utilitarianism makes no appeal to religion or belief in a god; this is important in trying to give good reasons for why we should act morally. Second, it emphasizes the importance of human happiness. However much people differ, they all want happiness in some form. Third, it is impartial and aims at improving the lot of most groups of human beings. Fourth, it argues that we can decide what to do by calculating the consequences. This may at times be difficult to do, but in principle it gives us a way of dealing with moral problems and choosing the right course of action.

❋ ❋ ❋SUMMARY ❋ ❋ ❋

● Bentham's utilitarianism: the rightness of an action depends on its utility, that is, its consequences in increasing or decreasing happiness. Increases and decreases in happiness are to be measured in amounts of pleasure and pain.

● Mill's utilitarianism took Bentham as a starting point.

● Mill thought that he could give a broader conception of utilitarianism by introducing the notion of quality in pleasures as well as quantity, emphasizing altruism and claiming that the other things that human beings value are valued because they contribute to happiness.

● Utilitarianism as a theory is plausible and attractive and has active supporters to this day.

Criticisms of utilitarianism

One of the reasons that Mill's *Utilitarianism* is a classic work in moral philosophy is, to put it in Mill's terms, the quantity and quality of discussion it led to. For much of the twentieth century, utilitarianism was strongly criticized by philosophers, but it has, along with Mill himself, had a revival in the last 30 years or so.

First though, there is a complaint that some people have made against utilitarianism in general. They say that it is just not possible to calculate pleasures or happiness in the way suggested. And if this criticism were correct, then utilitarianism could not even get started. To take up an example used earlier, reading a philosophy book cannot even be compared to drinking a bottle of champagne. It is not like being a judge at a dog show, where the judges have a set of agreed criteria by which to compare the dogs. Comparing dogs is comparing like with like. Comparing different pleasures is not at all the same thing.

This is exaggerated. In fact, we do quite a lot of comparing of different pleasures, for example, when I decide whether to spend the money I have left over at the end of the week on champagne or a philosophy book (they can both be obtained for about the same price). Another example of a difficult but necessary evaluation is deciding where to go for a family holiday. Different destinations will provide different combinations of pleasures and pains to parents and children of varying ages and tastes. It is no solution to say that, because the evaluation is virtually impossible, the family will not take a holiday this year!

PLEASURES

To turn to Mill's improvements to utilitarianism, his distinction between higher and lower pleasures has troubled many. His criterion, that those who have experienced both always choose the higher pleasure over the lower, has not seemed obvious to many critics. Does it work so simply? Most people in Britain have heard classical music at some point in their lives. Yet the majority continue to prefer popular music to classical. Mill attempted to strengthen his case by adding that those who can judge quality should be 'competently acquainted' with both. This might not be much help, however. There are many, more than competent, musicians (jazz musicians in particular) who prefer popular music to classical music. Similarly, it is perfectly plausible that someone who is a competent philosopher can get more actual pleasure from watching football matches.

Perhaps the problem here is that we are still talking in terms of 'pleasure'. We should remember that Mill also used terms like 'higher faculties'. By these, he seems to have had in mind things like intelligence, imagination, creativity. He wanted to contrast activity to passivity. This would appear to be the main difference between Socrates and the fool, and also between poetry and push-pin.

On the other hand, when we compare the lives of Socrates and the fool, are we comparing the amount of happiness within each life? Is it not rather that we are comparing different kinds of life for different kinds of character? In this case, it is hard to imagine anyone seriously faced with the choice between the two. Besides which, if Socrates was dissatisfied throughout his life, then it is hard to see that his life is the happier one.

And yet, even if the arguments are weak, there still seems to be something in what Mill is saying. He believes in a certain *fullness of life*. This is not a phrase he uses and what he says in *Utilitarianism* does not take us very far in understanding it, but by the time we have discussed all of this work, it will become clearer that he has an optimistic and inspiring view of the possible richness of human life.

ALTRUISM

Mill declared that provided happiness is maximized, we should be impartial between our own interests and those of other people. Some have thought this to be too demanding. It ignores the fact that we care more for some people than for others. The problem has been expressed in a puzzle that has come in different variations. Suppose you come to a house where a fire has started. Two people are in the house and are in danger of being trapped by the flames. There is only time to save one of them. As it happens, you recognize both people. One is a famous scientist, engaged in work that will benefit humanity (Einstein, say, or Stephen Hawking); the other is only the cleaner, but she happens to be your mother. Which one do you save? Utilitarianism will require you, so it is said, to rescue the scientist; but most people would want to save their mother. Perhaps they are wrong to want to do this. Generalizing from this, the criticism is made that utilitarianism neglects what is important to us as individuals.

INGREDIENTS OF HAPPINESS

Mill aimed to show that happiness is the one thing that is wanted purely for its own sake and that anything else that people want is actually wanted for the sake of their happiness. This at least is an improvement on Bentham's one-dimensional account of human psychology, for Mill is acknowledging the variety of ways in which human beings seek fulfilment in their lives. Mill is carrying out a balancing act here. On the one hand, he seems to be recognizing that human lives can have different purposes, interests and ideals. In this case, though, we might not need the concept of happiness. On the other hand, for utilitarianism to retain its value, it needs something which can function as the common denominator of what is good, otherwise we cannot evaluate the advantages of different courses of action. And happiness is the best candidate.

However, to some critics it has seemed that Mill is not so much balancing as trying to square the circle. He says that other values (such as virtue, music, money, power) are sought for their own sake *and* as ingredients of happiness. Is this claim based upon factual evidence? Now consider a miser, a man who pursues money for its own sake. It would appear that he gets no pleasure from his money, so would this not be a counter-example? Mill might reply that his desire for money for its own sake just shows that it is a 'part of happiness'. In other words 'being desired for its own sake' is regarded as *meaning* 'being desired as part of happiness'. But if these mean the same thing, then nothing is really sought for its own sake and Mill's attempt to broaden utilitarianism seems to be empty.

This is quite a tricky part of Mill's thought and philosophers have engaged in rather technical arguments over it. Some, however, have remained sympathetic to Mill. One suggestion is that he is thinking about happiness in a similar way to the Greek philosophers, especially Aristotle, who said that there is a single goal at which everyone aims. That goal is happiness, taken in a wide sense, and is linked to the exercise of all our faculties.

UTILITARIANISM IN GENERAL

Despite Mill's adaptations of Bentham's utilitarianism, there remain criticisms of all forms of this school of thought.

The classical objection is that there are moral principles which are at odds with utilitarianism. One specific claim is that it would permit unfairness in various ways. Utility would permit the sacrifice of one person or a few for the sake of the many. Suppose a grisly murder has taken place and there is a strong public demand for something to be done. The police have no suspects. Critics claim that utilitarianism would justify imprisoning or executing an innocent person, since sacrificing this one individual would promote the common good. The beneficial consequences would outweigh the injustice to that one person.

A similar kind of criticism is this. There are certain actions which we do because we ought to do them, not as a result of calculating the consequences. It is just the right thing to do to keep our promises, pay our debts and not tell lies.

It is not difficult to picture a case where breaking one's promise would create greater benefit. Suppose I am going somewhere and have promised to take my daughter on the back of my bicycle. As I am about to leave, my son says he wants to come along. I cannot take them both. Suppose also that my son would have greater pleasure from the trip than my daughter, even when taking into account my daughter's added disappointment. The utilitarian would say that I should take my son rather than my daughter. But this ignores the crucial difference between the alternatives, that I made a promise to my daughter.

Take the case of lying. A number of philosophers have firmly held that it is always prohibited. The German philosopher **Immanuel Kant** believed that it is prohibited even where a would-be murderer asks whether your friend, who is pursued by him, has taken refuge in your house. Utilitarianism would clearly justify lying to prevent this.

KEY FACT

Immanuel Kant (1724–1804): German philosopher. One of the great figures of Western philosophy.

Mill deals with problems like these by introducing a two-tier theory to describe how moral decisions are made. In his view there is an important role for moral principles or moral rules. The greatest happiness principle is still the fundamental principle of morality, but it is supported by subordinate principles, such as 'Killing the innocent is wrong', 'Keep your promises' and 'Lying is wrong'. Such moral rules, although secondary principles, contain, in Mill's view, the accumulated experience of humankind about which kinds of action will have good or bad consequences. Moral rules are 'landmarks and direction-points'. We speak the truth because the rule tells us to. The rule reminds us that the practice of truth-telling has good consequences.

So far so good. But how far does it take us? We have the rule, for example, that 'lying is wrong' and we have a specific occasion when an act of lying will do no harm and have good consequences. Do we follow the rule or think about the consequences of this particular act?

There has been a lot of debate about where Mill stands on this issue. There is what has been called rule-utilitarianism, which is the theory that we should be guided by a moral rule because it is the one which, if generally followed, will produce the best consequences. And there is what is known as act-utilitarianism. This recognizes the importance of rules, but sees them as 'rules of thumb', as convenient guidelines which can save time in working out whether a particular act is justified or not. Critics would add that if the moral rules have this status, then they can be too easily overturned for minor gains of pleasure or happiness, and not just in extreme cases.

We have to be cautious here. Mill was careful to claim that utilitarianism did not remove moral dilemmas and difficulties. 'There exists no moral system under which there do not arise unequivocal cases of conflicting obligation.' Utilitarianism at least gives us a way of dealing with them, as it does in the case where Kant seems to be of no help, when faced with the would-be murderer.

JIM IN SOUTH AMERICA

The most sophisticated attack on utilitarianism in recent years has come from the eminent British philosopher, Bernard Williams. He presented this scenario: Jim is on a botanical expedition in South America. On entering a small town he finds that 20 Indians are about to be executed by a group of soldiers. The captain of the soldiers welcomes Jim as an honoured visitor and suggests that, to mark the occasion, Jim himself should shoot one of the Indians, and the other 19 will be set free. If Jim refuses, all 20 will be shot.

What should he do? As we saw earlier in this chapter, utilitarianism can have as a rule 'do not kill innocent people'. Yet we can also see that there are utilitarian reasons for killing the innocent hostage. Williams is not necessarily presenting this as a counter-example. He is asking us to consider the reasoning that is applied to the case. If we apply only utilitarian reasoning, that is the calculation of which course of action is going to have the most beneficial or, in this case, the least harmful consequences, then we will be leaving out something very important. This is Jim's feeling of moral responsibility. If he takes the utilitarian choice of killing one Indian, he will be responsible for a person's death. Williams is claiming that utilitarianism leaves no place for what he calls 'integrity' in the sense of the value to be found in a person 'sticking by what he regards as ethically necessary and worthwhile', as he puts it.

This integrity and the commitments that go with it are not things that go into the balance of calculation about ensuring happiness or avoiding happiness. They have a much deeper place in our lives than that. To think as a utilitarian in Jim's position would be to damage, even destroy, his moral integrity. There is no reason why Jim, in his awful dilemma, should think in utilitarian terms of 'the greatest happiness'.

This emphasis on the importance of Jim's own moral integrity in this situation has appeared suspect to many philosophers. Unfortunately, to discuss it further would take us beyond the limits of what can be done here.

THE BALANCE SHEET
In this chapter several criticisms have been made against utilitarianism. The strongest ones claim that utilitarianism is not of much value for individuals having to choose courses of action. Bentham was, in fact, more interested in questions of legislation and public action. He proposed utilitarianism principally as a guide to public policy makers. Seen in this way, as a standard for public rather than private choice, the greatest happiness principle is more resilient to the usual objections. It comes into its own in public situations. Since the actions of a government or organization will affect people in different ways, the right action is the one which increases the happiness of all those affected by the action.

This point can be strengthened by another consideration. It may be that happiness is difficult to attain and that we are uncertain about what it is. But suffering and hardship are more easily recognized. Both Bentham and Mill thought that the first aim of utilitarianism should be to alleviate what Mill calls the 'positive evils of life', such as poverty and disease. It is hard to argue with that as a starting-point.

✹ ✹ ✹ SUMMARY ✹ ✹ ✹

Critics have raised a number of problems with utilitarianism:

● It is not possible to compare pleasures in the way that utilitarianism requires.

● Mill's distinction between higher and lower pleasures cannot be justified.

● Utilitarianism is too altruistic.

● Mill is not convincing in his claim that everything people pursue in their lives leads to happiness.

● We have moral rules which utilitarianism would have us reject when it suits us. (In reply Mill has a two-tier theory, which gives a place to moral rules.)

● Utilitarianism neglects the importance of personal commitments in making moral choices.

The liberal 5

The most highly regarded of Mill's works today is probably his long essay *On Liberty*, written in close cooperation with his wife and published in 1859 shortly after her death. This was the same year that another revolutionary work was published, Charles Darwin's *The Origin of Species*.

Mill's book was something of a best seller. The first edition sold out quickly and a second appeared later in the same year. It was immediately controversial. Most of the reviews were critical. Some even claimed that the arguments it contained were subversive and posed a threat to social order in Britain. However, the book's sales show that Mill had enthusiastic readers.

On Liberty is still regarded as a classic statement of the case for individual liberty. And besides its classic status, it is a *living* work. Mill's arguments in this essay provide a framework within which to discuss the question of how free we should be to live as we please. His arguments are the starting point for many contemporary debates: pornography, the wearing of seat-belts, decriminalization of soft drugs, euthanasia, laws regulating sexual conduct and so on.

Mill's concern at the time of writing *On Liberty* was, however, about the way that Victorian society might go. By the middle of the nineteenth century the belief that democracy was the best form of government had become well established in Britain and America. Mill certainly believed this, but he was also worried that it might also become an oppressive form of government. He feared that if, as must happen in a democracy, the majority have power, this could lead to the majority exercising a tyranny over the minority. The majority might say that everyone within society should agree with them or at least not express any disagreement. There would be strong social pressure to conform. Mill wanted to speak up for minorities and for individuals. Against conformity he praised being different – different in opinion, different in lifestyle.

Mill feared the spread of a Victorian middle-class notion of respectability, reinforced by a very conformist Christianity. He gives the example of a man who was sentenced to 21 months' imprisonment 'for uttering, and writing on a gate, some offensive words concerning Christianity.' One of the early reviews of his book argued that a Christian state, like Britain, had the right to prohibit atheism.

A similar conformity dominated American society for a time in the 1950s. An American Senator, Joe McCarthy, took advantage of American anxieties in the Cold War and launched an attack on what he called 'un-American activities'. Any criticism of America could be given this label and thus silenced. It was a way of stifling radical ideas and establishing conformity of opinion.

THE HARM PRINCIPLE

Mill, therefore, wished to safeguard the freedom of the individual against society. How could social pressure be resisted? His answer was to argue that, for each member of society, there should be an area of freedom from constraint. There were some things society should not interfere with. He proposed what he called his 'very simple principle': 'the only purpose for which power can be rightfully exercised over any member of a civilized community, against this will, is to prevent harm to others.' This has come to be called the 'harm principle'. Only when there is a risk of harm to others is there any justification for intervention.

One of the controversial topics in modern societies is whether soft drugs should be decriminalized. Many people use soft drugs, many more do not but accept their use by others, and many think they are dangerous and should remain illegal. The argument in favour of decriminalization is that if people wish to use soft drugs for their private purposes then this should be permitted. If the use of soft drugs harms anybody, it will only harm the person who uses them.

Probably the most significant use of Mill's harm principle since the mid-twentieth century has been in attitudes to sexual morality. As late as 1948 in America there were arrests for adultery. However, in 2001 an entertainer like George Melly can describe to the audience of Radio 4 (a mainstream British radio station) that he went to bed with a married couple and justify it like this: 'I hold to the principle that you can do what you want so long as no one gets hurt.'

There has also been a huge change in attitudes to homosexuality. Until 1967 it was illegal in Britain. Homosexuals were a minority who had to keep their sexual preferences hidden from the rest of society. They were a minority required to conform to the views of the majority. Eventually it was recognized that homosexual acts between 'consenting adults in private' harmed no one else and it became possible to change the law, so that homosexuality was no longer illegal for men over 21. Even after this change, many homosexuals felt social pressure to hide their sexuality, and even now they might not be as free as other people to live in the way they wish to, for example, in rural communities.

'The only freedom which deserves the name is that of pursuing our own good in our own way', writes Mill. This means that society or government has to justify any interference in our lives. This includes interference 'for our own good'. Mill was strongly opposed to what is called 'paternalism', the assertion that society knows what is good for the individual and can legislate accordingly. In cases where there is a risk of harm to the individual concerned, we can argue or plead with him or her, attempt to persuade them not to do what they are doing. But we cannot compel or coerce the person.

There are, it must be said, exceptions to the harm principle. First, children and young people. Second, those such as the certified insane, who need to be cared for by others. There is a third and more controversial category. Mill thought it acceptable to use coercion in 'backward states of society' for their own good, 'backward' meaning societies with low levels of education.

IMPORTANCE OF INDIVIDUALITY

Mill presents his harm principle in the early part of *On Liberty*. He follows this with a discussion of freedom of opinion, which is covered in Chapter 7; and then with a discussion of freedom in how we live, which is the topic of this section.

It is not just that the majorities should leave minorities and individuals alone. Mill has a more positive argument. Given this freedom, this 'space' so to speak, we should use it for our own development. Where it does not affect others 'individuality should assert itself'. Mill calls for 'the free development of individuality'. We should be free to conduct our own 'experiments in living', to adopt our own 'mode or plan of life'. Mill is emphasizing the value of self-development and what might be called, in a modern phrase, 'living your own life'.

This attitude is widely accepted in Western societies and might be thought to be obvious. However, when we remind ourselves of the conformist age in which it was written, when all were expected to accept the doctrines of the Church of England, where men were likely to follow the occupations of their fathers, where a woman's only career was that of housewife, then Mill was being very radical.

One writer of the time had worried, like Mill, that the citizens of a democracy would turn into 'industrious sheep'. And perhaps Mill's arguments can also be applied to the modern age, for it has its own sheep-like characteristics, for example, when large numbers of people watch the same television programmes and films and buy the same products from the same shops.

Thus, we see Mill making a close link between individuality and development. He wanted to see the development of all the human faculties – 'of perception, judgement, discriminative feeling, mental activity and moral choice.' Here the reader is reminded of what he said in *Utilitarianism* about exercising the human faculties. But what he goes on to say in *On Liberty* is even more ambitious. A human being, by cultivating all that is individual in him or herself, becomes 'a noble and beautiful object of contemplation'.

FREEDOM'S GOOD CONSEQUENCES

What does Mill say to support his view that we should have a space to ourselves, an area of freedom for each responsible adult in a civilized society?

What he does *not* say is that we have a natural right to freedom. Most talk about freedoms at the present time makes claims about individuals' rights. For Mill, however, any talk of rights must be based on utilitarian grounds. To claim a right to freedom, for Mill, means that preserving our freedom will tend to increase happiness. 'I regard utility as the ultimate appeal on all ethical questions; but it must be utility in the largest sense, grounded on the permanent interests of man as a progressive being.' It is not very clear what exactly this last part of the sentence means, but Mill does go on to say something about the good consequences of preserving individual liberty.

First, he says that if we allow individuals to develop their faculties and abilities, we can learn from them, for it is they who often make new discoveries.

Second, if we have such developed individuals in society, society will be run more effectively. These individuals will act as a defence against uninformed public opinion and 'collective mediocrity'. They will guide the majority with their advice and influence. Mill once again seems elitist here, for he seems to be suggesting an intelligentsia that would lead opinion in the right direction. Nevertheless he does add the comment that nonconformity and even eccentricity are useful in simply not conforming to the tyranny of opinion.

A third reason Mill gives for individual liberty is that it is bad for everyone in society to be dominated by stereotypes. He writes: 'there is no reason that all human existence should be constructed on some one or small number of patters.' And here he too uses the metaphor of sheep. 'Human beings are not like sheep, and even sheep are not indistinguishably alike.' In short, all of us need diversity to lead a fuller life.

Lastly, not only do we need the individuality that encourages social improvement; we need it to avoid social stagnation. If the 'despotism of custom' were to take complete control, society would become completely stationary and then go into decline. Mill claimed that this is what had happened to the countries of the Far East, specifically China, which had remained stationary for thousands of years. 'They have succeeded beyond all hope ... in making a people all alike, all governing their thoughts and conduct by the same maxims and rules.' Whether this is fair to the China of the nineteenth century is a question for historians. However, the criticism of trying to govern a people's thoughts might well be applied to the countries of Eastern Europe under the stifling influence of Communism.

THE INDIVIDUAL AND SOCIETY

For all his praise of liberty, Mill is careful to stress that this liberty must not injure others. Individuality should be cultivated 'within the limits imposed by the rights and interests of others'. Mill believed that there should be a balance between the individual and the society around him or her, but he was worried that society had got the better of the individual. He also suggested that each of us has a social part of his or her nature which should be developed at the expense of the selfish part.

This is rather vague and, as a good philosopher, Mill is not content to leave things there. He spends the last two chapters of *On Liberty* discussing in detail the boundaries between the individual and society.

Throughout he uses a distinction between actions that concern only the individual and those which concern others – between 'self-regarding acts' and 'other-regarding acts'. Self-regarding acts do not harm others. You may not like what I am doing, but this does not count as 'harm'. There has to be some 'perceptible damage'. I might be a fool, a liar, cruel, malicious, bad-tempered. You would be quite right to disapprove of these and avoid my company, but you should not interfere with me, unless I am harming others. If I spend all my money on drink or gambling I am harming only myself. Of course, if I have a family, then I am harming them and that is a different matter.

Not surprisingly, Mill disapproved of laws to regulate drinking. At the time Mill was writing, the sale of alcohol was prohibited in half the states of the USA. Furthermore, 'prohibition', as it was called, was introduced in America in the 1920s and turned out to be a dismal failure. Mill called such temperance laws 'gross usurpations upon the liberty of private life'. His own view of drinking is not in question. Undoubtedly he would have thought, as we saw when discussing his utilitarianism, that it was one of the lower pleasures and played no part in the development of a man or woman's higher faculties. A philosopher who can write of human beings as becoming 'a noble and beautiful object of contemplation' will not look approvingly at someone who spends all of their days in the pub. But still, this is what the individual has chosen to do, it is not harming anyone else and he should be left alone to do it.

✳ ✳ ✳ SUMMARY ✳ ✳ ✳

● Mill uses his 'very simple principle', that is, the 'harm principle', to mark off a space for the freedom of the individual. This space allows individuals to develop themselves and thus become better human beings. This, in turn, is a benefit to the society of which they are part. 'The worth of a State, in the long run, is the worth of the individuals composing it.'

● In his *Autobiography*, Mill described *On Liberty* as 'a kind of philosophic text-book of a single truth, which the changes progressively taking place in modern society tend to bring out into ever stronger relief: the importance, to man and society, of a large variety in types of character, and of giving full freedom to human nature to expand itself in innumerable and conflicting directions'.

6 Criticisms of the harm principle

On Liberty ran into criticisms from the moment it was published. Some of these were knee-jerk reactions of conservatives who were jolted by Mill's radicalism and, especially, his forceful remarks on Christianity. Others, though, took a more thoughtful approach and raised pointed questions about Mill's harm principle. Four important criticisms will be dealt with in this chapter.

WHAT IS HARM?

To put Mill's principle to work, we need to have a clear idea of what he meant by 'harm'. Chambers Dictionary defines the word as 'injury, physical, mental or moral' which is a wide definition. It looks as if Mill means to include physical harm, but there is a point that we have to bear in mind. People get hurt playing rugby or boxing. Might this be a reason for banning either sport? No, because if those taking part have given their 'free and informed consent', as the phrase goes, then they cannot be harmed in the relevant sense, provided that any injuries which occur (as they undoubtedly will in a boxing match) do so within the rules of the game.

And what about moral injury? What if you deeply offend my feelings – does this count? We shall discuss a case of this later in the chapter. Can harm be done only to individuals, or can it also be done to institutions and even ways of life?

Such questions, however, show that Mill's account is incomplete, not that it is flawed.

IS MILL TOO RADICAL?

Lord Devlin, a British High Court Judge, observed around 1960 that, on the face of it, suicide, abortion, euthanasia, duelling and incest between brother and sister 'are all acts which can be done in private and without offence to others'. Therefore, they would be permitted by the harm principle. At that time all of these were illegal and the writer quoted these as cases which society obviously could not tolerate.

The interesting thing about this list is that the first two items are no longer illegal. The third, euthanasia, is a subject for active debate and has been legalized in Holland. There is probably no pressure group for the restoration of duelling. It may have been banned because it led to people's death, an extreme form of harm, so to speak. Might incest be legalized by the mid-twenty-first century?

The case of soft drugs was mentioned in the previous chapter. What about hard drugs? If someone takes heroin, this need not affect anyone else, so why should we interfere by making heroin illegal?

Mill does give one example of a case where he would allow interference with the individual. It is permissible, he says, to prevent a man from crossing a river when we know, but he does not, that the bridge he is about to use is unsafe. 'They might seize him and turn him back, without any real infringement of his liberty; for liberty consists in doing what one desires, and he does not desire to fall into the river.'

The coercion is justified here because the man going towards the bridge does not have enough knowledge of the dangers ahead of him for us to be sure that he knows what he is doing. Otherwise, Mill believed that we should not interfere with what people decide to do 'with the full use of the reflecting faculty' (that is, their reason). This rather implies that he thought most people most of the time knew what they were doing. As he stressed a number of times, each of us is the best judge of our own interests.

But are we? Are we always making full use of our 'reflective faculty'? Mill made a distinction between children and adults. However, to be a fully mature, thinking adult is a considerable achievement. Many, if not most of us, have parts of our character which cause us to behave in immature or irrational ways. One of the important gains of the twentieth century has been greater knowledge of psychological forces that prevent us from acting fully rationally. In short, individuals do not always know what they are doing.

DOES EVERYTHING THAT WE DO AFFECT OTHER PEOPLE?

Mill's harm principle says that we can only interfere with people's liberty if they risk harming *other* people by their action. He made a distinction between two kinds of action, those which concern only myself – 'self-regarding actions' – and those which concern others – 'other-regarding actions'.

Critics have claimed, against Mill, that this distinction is not possible, for nearly all of our actions affect other people, even those actions which are apparently self-regarding. For example, if I decide to drink tea rather than coffee, this apparently trivial choice does have an effect on others. I am reducing the income of coffee producers and importers. To turn to more significant examples, heavy smokers contaminate the air for others. Even if they smoke only in the privacy of their own home, they increase the risk of a serious illness. This in turn will mean that they will be a strain on the health service. The same point could be made against heavy drinkers, with the addition that they set a bad example to others. In other words, Mill is wrong to assume that there are human actions which do not have social consequences.

This is, however, a very sweeping generalization. If it were to be followed, this would mean that we had no area of privacy at all. And, to remain with the example of drinking, if I live alone, without dependants, the only person who is harmed if I get drunk is myself.

The situation is somewhat different if I do this in a country where alcohol is banned. In that case I may give offence to many people. My apparently self-regarding action becomes other-regarding. But can I be said to have harmed their interests *in a significant way*? It does not look as if I have.

This mention of the notion of 'offence' brings us back to the first question raised in this chapter – what does Mill mean by 'harm'? Does it include what the dictionary called 'moral injury'? To offend people might count as a harm, and so be liable to prevention. But it is quite clear that Mill wanted a space for liberty that was not affected by what he called the mere 'likings and dislikings' of society. But then, would the harm principle allow offensive behaviour in public, such as a National Front march, parading Nazi symbols in a Jewish quarter? Some supporters of Mill have become worried at this point and have thought that the harm principle needs the addition of another principle to cover cases of public offence.

This discussion of self-regarding and other-regarding actions highlights the individual in relation to society. There are wider implications here. As the poet John Donne said, 'no man is an island.' In his reaction against the social conformity of his day, Mill supported · the individual. Perhaps he went too far.

Critics of Mill have argued that if we have a society along the lines that he suggests, people will only be interested in their own self-development and neglect their responsibilities and duties to the society of which they are part. Living in our own private spaces, we risk losing our attachment to the customs, cultures and traditions of our societies. To prevent this, there must be some acknowledgement of a shared morality. Thus, people might be right to be deeply offended by behaviour they disapprove of and right to attempt to restrain it.

We are now getting a long way from *On Liberty*, but I mention this debate because it is one that is active in modern philosophy. On one side are liberals, in the tradition of Mill, who stress the civil and political freedoms of the individual, on the other are communitarians, who stress the social nature of life, the ties of affection, kinship and the importance of a common purpose and tradition.

LIBERTY AND UTILITARIANISM

In the previous chapter we saw that Mill had utilitarian reasons for promoting the liberty of the individual. Liberty of the individual would lead to greater happiness, for himself and for society. On the other hand, Mill does seem to value freedom for its own sake very highly. Now, what of cases where people would be happier if they had less freedom?

One Victorian critic argued from a firmly pessimistic viewpoint. Fitzjames Stephen (who was also a utilitarian) said that 'there are and always will be in the world an enormous mass of bad and indifferent people.' How would they be helped by being given the freedom of which Mill speaks? Their 'experiments in living' are much more likely to be failures, with damage caused to the people around them. The only way they could be improved would be by compulsion and restraint. As one writer has pointed out, Mill thought of liberty as 'bracing and invigorating, because it fosters strong characters and promotes progress'. But what if it leads to idleness, drunkenness and long hours in front of the television?

This comes back to a point made in the discussion of whether Mill's principle is too radical. Perhaps he takes it for granted that we can easily become truly rational and mature adults. How do we decide between Mill's optimism and the pessimism of his critics on this question, that is, to what extent are people improved by being given more freedom? To the pessimist who stresses the weakness of humankind, Mill might reply that if they have compulsion and restraint applied to them, they have no chance whatever of improvement. It would be to treat them almost as slaves. The pessimistic attitude here is reminiscent of that of white South Africans who maintained the system of apartheid over the black majority in their country. The whites assumed that the blacks were incapable of self-improvement and so had to be subjected to compulsion and restraint.

Still, if the empirical evidence were to show that people were better off with less freedom, Mill would not be able to assert a utilitarian justification for his harm principle. Nevertheless he could still maintain that liberty was good in itself and so should be pursued.

There is another consideration here. In the last chapter, Mill's remark about man as a progressive being was quoted. I referred to it as a vague phrase. One plausible interpretation, though, is that Mill is claiming that men and women are capable of being educated. Mill believed in the possibilities of education – and most hardened pessimists, in the present age at least, do not disapprove of the fact that we educate our children nor of the claim that education should be universal in the world.

Imagine two schools. One works its students very hard. It is a very efficient machine for cramming its students with relevant information. It sticks rigorously to the curriculum and has little time for extra-curricular activities. This school gets very good exam results. A second school gets less good results, it takes a more relaxed line with them, but it encourages its pupils to think for themselves. In the longer term – at university or in the wider world – which school's pupils will do best?

✻ ✻ ✻ SUMMARY ✻ ✻ ✻

• In this chapter we discuss four important criticisms of Mill's harm principle.

• What does Mill mean by 'harm'? Perhaps the principle is not as clear as Mill thinks it is.

• Is Mill's principle too radical?

• Is it true that there are actions which do not affect other people?

• Is there a clash between the high value Mill gives to liberty and his utilitarianism?

7 On free speech

There is yet one more area in which *On Liberty* is still an important work.

Everyday in many countries, especially in North America and Europe, newspapers criticize the government, no matter which political party is in power. Whoever is Prime Minister will come under attack for one thing or another. What is more, this ability of the Press and individual citizens to comment on matters of public concern is taken for granted. Whether we agree with the criticism or not, we think it right that the criticism can be made openly. Yet it has not always been like this, nor is it like this all over the world. In the 1930s in the USSR, criticism of the leader Josef Stalin could condemn the speaker to several years in a Siberian labour camp. In Burma, in the year 2000, people have been given prison sentences for handing out leaflets that attack the country's military government and call for democracy.

Freedom of speech, then, is a key value in modern democracies. President Roosevelt, speaking during the Second World War, called it one of the 'four essential freedoms' for which the allies were fighting against Germany and Japan. (The four are freedom of speech and religion, freedom from want and fear.) Freedom of speech was then recognized by the United Nations in the 1948 Declaration of Human Rights and, more recently, in the European Convention of Human Rights.

Freedom of speech, however, is not just concerned with politics. It allows people to comment on and criticize institutions like the police or the armed forces or large companies, such as Microsoft or Shell. Churches have been very powerful institutions. For several centuries, if any one expressed an opinion that was different from the established doctrine of the Roman Catholic church, it would be condemned as heresy, and might be punished by burning at the stake. In 1988 the

British writer Salman Rushdie published a novel, *The Satanic Verses*, which some Muslims believed insulted the founder of their religion, Muhammed. Death threats were made and Rushdie was forced into hiding.

So, in the West at least, freedom of speech is generally thought to be a good thing. But it is not enough to simply assert this. What are the reasons for valuing freedom of speech and claiming it as a right for all human beings?

The most thorough case in favour of freedom of speech was made by Mill in the second chapter of *On Liberty*, which has the title 'Of the liberty of thought and discussion'. He gives us the classic argument and, though it is only one chapter of the larger work, it is important in its own right.

Early in this chapter Mill declares forthrightly: 'If all mankind minus one were of one opinion, and only one person were of the contrary opinion, mankind would be no more justified in silencing that one person, than he, if he had the power, would be justified in silencing mankind.' This is a very strong statement, especially when we discover that Mill means it to apply even if the opinion of that one person is wrong, for example, that the earth is flat. So why should no opinion, whether right or wrong, be suppressed? Because, it would be, according to Mill 'robbing the human race'. He goes on: 'If the opinion is right, they are deprived of the opportunity of exchanging error for truth: if wrong, they lose, what is almost as great a benefit, the clearer perception and livelier impression of truth, produced by its collision with error.'

In short, Mill believes that freedom of opinion will lead to truth.

WHEN THE DISSENTING OPINION IS TRUE

We can see the clash between majority and minority opinion in the famous case of Galileo. He was condemned by the Roman Catholic Church for putting forward the true opinion that the earth goes round the sun. This went against the widely held belief, supported by the Church, that the earth was the centre of the universe. Had it been possible to completely suppress Galileo's theory, our understanding of the universe, provided by Galileo himself and later by Newton and Einstein, would not have been possible.

Of course, if one opinion is firmly held by a majority of people and a different opinion is put forward, the majority is very unlikely to recognize its truth. It is one thing, though, to deny the contrary opinion; it is a far more serious step to want to *suppress* that opinion. In this case, says Mill, the suppressors are making 'an assumption of infallibility'. They are insisting that they can never be wrong. They assume that 'their certainty is the same thing as absolute certainty.'

It is easy to show that human history is full of beliefs that were held by a large majority of people and have since been discarded, for one reason or another. Two have been mentioned already, that the earth is flat and that it is the centre of the universe. Here is another, from Mill's own time. A critic of Mill wrote of 'the natural aristocracy of Man over Woman … this natural incapacity of Woman to become the rival and competitor, however well fitted to be the partner and helpmate of Man.' Again, some may still believe this, but it would not now be asserted so complacently, as if it were an obvious truth.

This is not to say that it is wrong to have beliefs about which we feel certain. Mill is not criticizing this: 'It is not the feeling sure of a doctrine … which I call the assumption of infallibility. It is the undertaking to decide that question for others' – by suppressing any contrary opinion and not allowing others to consider it.

If history shows that human beings very often get things wrong, if they are in fact so *fallible*, how then do we ever get to the truth? Mill's discussion now becomes subtle and fruitful. He puts forward a convincing view of how knowledge is attained. It is due to 'a quality of the human mind, the source of everything respectable in man either as an intellectual or a moral being, namely, that his errors are corrigible. He is capable of rectifying his mistakes by discussion and experience.' Experience on its own is not enough; discussion is also needed to bring the relevant facts and arguments forward, to show how experience is to be evaluated. Mill sketches an attractive picture of individual men and women with open minds, prepared to consider a range of opinions (as permitted by freedom of speech) in their approach to knowledge and truth.

'The only way in which a human being can make some approach to knowing the whole of a subject, is by hearing what can be said about it by persons of every variety of opinion, and studying all modes in which it can be looked at by every character of mind. No wise man ever acquired his wisdom in any mode but this; nor is it in the nature of human intellect to become wise in any other manner.'

The clarity and firmness of Mill's language are invigorating. At moments like this philosophy becomes deeply inspiring.

WHEN THE DISSENTING OPINION IS FALSE

So far most readers will be sympathetic to Mill's argument, for most people have a prejudice in favour of truth against falsity. However why give support or space to opinions that are wrong? Because, as mentioned earlier, Mill holds that even if the dissenting opinion is wrong, it should not be suppressed. He now pursues his argument in a bold and challenging way.

The phrase he used at the beginning of his discussion was 'the clearer perception and livelier impression of truth'. Mill wants to argue that false opinions have a valuable function. How do they manage this?

Mill deals with this question by developing his emphasis on the value of open discussion. In his view, it is not enough for me to hold a true opinion, I should also be aware of the reasons for holding that opinion and of the alternatives to it: 'He who knows only his own side of the case, knows little of that.' If I cannot give reasons why I hold a particular belief, then what is my belief based on? It may come from authority, I believe it because I have been told to do so: for example, that Charles Dickens is a great writer, even though I have never read any of his novels. Or it may come from inclination, I believe it because it suits me: Dickens is a great writer, simply because I *have* read his novels, but no one else's. If I cannot give good reasons myself, then 'This is not knowing the truth. Truth, thus held, is but one superstition the more.'

Mill has a further point to make. Open discussion, he claims, keeps alive the meaning of the majority opinion. Even if true, it can degenerate into an empty dogma if it is not questioned. In Britain and many countries it is pretty well taken for granted that democracy is the best political system. Nevertheless a democracy that is aware of its weaknesses (and is made aware through public criticism) will be a healthier democracy than one which assumes it is perfect.

WHEN THE DISSENTING OPINION IS PARTLY TRUE, PARTLY FALSE

Although he does not mention it at the beginning of the chapter, Mill also introduces a third possibility, which he thinks is more common than either of the two he has been discussing, that the contrary or dissenting opinion is a mixture of truth and falsity. It is no surprise that Mill welcomes this too: 'Truth', he writes, 'in the great practical concerns of life, is a question of the reconciling and combining of opposites … only through a diversity of opinion is there, in the existing state of human intellect, a chance of fair play to all sides of the truth.'

DISSENTING WITH MILL

To sum up, for Mill, freedom of speech is the open expression of opinion. Open expression of opinion is necessary for the wide-ranging discussion or 'collision of opinions' which makes possible the achievement of knowledge and truth. So we must tolerate dissent.

Disagreement with Mill can take two directions. First, as we have seen previously, some would say that he is too optimistic. They would say that society as a whole is just not capable of the rational process of considering a range of opinions and achieving a correct choice through discussion. Society often has to be guided. As authoritarian governments and institutions like to claim: 'leave matters to us; we know best.'

It is certainly true that Mill's argument works best in the context of a society that has achieved good standards of education. But he would add that the free expression of opinion is a means of educating society. Furthermore, any country which claims to be a democracy has to have some faith in the reasoning powers of its citizens who, in the end, are the ones who decide. Also, it is now a common practice, in democratic societies, to deal with some issues in public policy by actively seeking a wide range of opinions. One recent British example is cloning, where scientists, philosophers, and representatives of different religions were invited to give their views.

A second line of disagreement is perhaps that Mill goes too far. If speech is given too much freedom, it might cause harm in unacceptable ways. It is already limited in some areas: we have laws of libel and slander, which restrict what can be said about other people; governments can prevent reporting on matters of 'national security'. A trickier case concerns the Holocaust. In Germany and Austria it is illegal to disseminate writings which deny that it took place and there have been suggestions that a similar law should be introduced in Britain. It certainly seems that Mill's argument would permit Holocaust denial. Yet it is very difficult to see how such material, which flies in the face of the huge amount of evidence for the Holocaust, can be considered a genuine contribution to a debate aiming at knowledge and truth, while its existence causes a lot of offence and distress.

Then there are issues that have arisen with the development of modern media, which Mill could not be aware of, and which seem to exploit freedom of speech, such as Press intrusion into people's private lives and pornography. How far are these to be permitted?

Newspapers excuse their intrusions (which usually seem to be about the sex lives of politicians) on the grounds of 'public interest'. There is no doubt that the public are 'interested', but is it 'in the public interest' that we should know whether this or that politician has had an affair with this or that actress (or actor, come to that)? Mill's argument could be used against this sort of intrusion: it is not in the public interest if it does not give knowledge that the public needs.

On the question of pornography Mill, as a high-minded Victorian liberal, would probably have been horrified by the amount of pornography that is available. Could he use his argument here? In fact, I think he can. For it is difficult to see how pornography is a contribution to any discussion that might lead to knowledge and truth; if it is not, then it could be suppressed. But still, Mill might not be happy with this, given that he is largely in favour of tolerance rather than suppression.

These criticisms all deserve, as Mill would be glad to admit, further discussion. However, it can reasonably be claimed that Mill's argument does set out a strong case. He shows the value of freedom of speech, which seems all the stronger in the pluralistic and multicultural societies of the twenty-first century. He at least establishes what philosophers call the burden of proof: we should have freedom of speech unless there are good reasons otherwise in particular circumstances. As one recent writer commented, Mill's achievement is to have put forward 'the historically astonishing principle that public disagreement is a creative force'.

* * *SUMMARY* * *

As Mill summarized his own argument:

- 'We have now recognized the necessity to the mental well-being of mankind (on which all their other well-being depends) of freedom of opinion, and freedom of the expression of opinion, on four distinct grounds; which we will now briefly recapitulate.

- First, if any opinion is compelled to silence, that opinion may, for aught we can certainly know, be true. To deny this is to assume our infallibility.

- Secondly, though the silenced opinion be an error, it may, and very commonly does, contain a portion of the truth; and since the general or prevailing opinion on any subject is rarely or never the whole truth, it is only by the collision of adverse opinions that the remainder of the truth has any chance of being supplied.

- Thirdly, even if the received opinion be not only true, but the whole truth; unless it is suffered to be, and actually is, vigorously and earnestly contested, it will, by most of those who receive it, be held in the manner of a prejudice, with little comprehension of its rational grounds.

- Fourthly, the meaning of the doctrine itself will be in danger of being lost, or enfeebled, and deprived of its vital effect on the character and conduct: the dogma becoming a mere formal profession, inefficacious for good, but cumbering the ground, and preventing the growth of any real and heartfelt conviction, from reason or personal experience.'

- There are two lines of disagreement with Mill's argument: first, that he is too optimistic about people's rationality; second, that he is too permissive in what he allows.

8 The feminist

As mentioned in Chapter 2, Mill was probably the first to suggest in the House of Commons that women as well as men should have the vote. His proposal, in a debate on new legislation for extending the vote, was that the word 'man' should be replaced by the word 'person'.

Now, to return to *On Liberty* for a moment. One of Mill's main targets in that book was social conformity. Some critics were shocked by his views. Others, though, tried to disarm his radicalism by claiming that he was making a mountain out of a molehill. He was, they said, exaggerating the extent of social conformity; people in British society did actually have the freedom he called for. Such comments in fact show how blinkered they were. Mill's arguments for liberty were for all 'persons' or 'individuals', not just men, a point which hardly any of his first readers recognized. This only became evident when he published *The Subjection of Women* in 1869, two years after that debate in parliament, and some eight years after he had written it.

The Subjection of Women aroused more antagonism than anything Mill ever wrote, yet two editions of the book quickly sold out. This time not only his enemies, but his friends were horrified. One admirer of *On Liberty* called this latest work 'rank moral and social anarchy'. An always stern critic of Mill was Fitzjames Stephen, already quoted in Chapter 6. Here is his horrified reaction to *The Subjection of Women*:

'Are boys and girls to be educated indiscriminately, and to be instructed in the same things? Are boys to learn to sew, to keep house, and to cook, and girls to play at cricket, to row, and to be drilled like boys? I cannot argue with a person who says "yes". A person who says "no" admits an inequality between the sexes on which education must be founded, and which it must therefore perpetuate and perhaps increase.'

Also among Mill's critics were a number of women who accepted the status quo. They claimed that, the ideal woman was man's helpmate, that most women saw marriage as their liberty, that women were different from men, and being physically weaker by nature, they could not be equal.

THE SUBJECTION OF WOMEN

Although, in Britain, much of what Mill argued for has taken place, there is still good reason for reading his book. In the first place, in most of the countries of the world, women are expected to be subservient to men. This hardly needs illustration, but the most recent example of it I have come across is this: a woman who recently visited Namibia in Africa was asked by her guide, who spoke English, to explain what was to him a deeply puzzling phrase 'Ladies first'. At the same time, as more and more women go out to work, all around the world, they are transforming their own societies. It has recently been argued that the equality and education of women is the most important force for promoting democracy and economic development in poorer countries.

Second, the book is a model of crisp argument and an excellent example of how to use reason to confront deeply held prejudices in a society. Mill takes the generalizations and clichés about women and deals with them one by one so that the interwoven beliefs are taken apart and the prejudices collapse.

The solidarity of the prejudice against Mill means that he has to work harder to shift it, and this is one of the reasons why the book is considerably longer than *Utilitarianism* or *On Liberty*. The fact that prejudice is supported only by feeling, makes it all the more difficult to argue against. As Mill says, the natural inferiority of women is an 'almost universal opinion'. This means that the burden of proof is upon all those who would change that opinion.

Mill's fundamental aim, he says in his first paragraph, is to attack the legal subordination of women. It is both wrong in itself and a great hindrance to human improvement: 'it ought to be replaced by a principle of perfect equality admitting no power or privilege on the one side, nor disability on the other.'

DISMANTLING PREJUDICE

This first part of *The Subjection of Women* is largely concerned with Mill's dismantling of the justifications for the subjection of women. It had of course always been the usual state of affairs. According to its supporters, the fact that it was customary meant that experience had shown that it was the best arrangement. Mill would accept this, he said, if any other arrangement besides male domination had been tried out. But as there had not, the argument from experience did not apply. In fact, the subjection of women was a development of the primitive situation where a woman, being physically weaker, was tied to some man. Mill then tellingly makes a comparison with slavery. Slaves were initially acquired by force. Slavery was then supported by legislation; it was several hundred years before anyone questioned it. (The law abolishing Britain's involvement in the slave trade had come into force in 1808, but the American Civil War of 1861–65, fought over the issue of slavery, would have been fresh in reader's minds.) Mill adroitly turns this argument from custom around and says that it is nothing more than the law of the strongest, that might is right.

Yes, say the proponents of women's inferiority, but the rule of men is different because women consent to it. This is simply not true, Mill replies, for a great number of women do not accept their lot. Many are calling for better education and to have admission to a wide range of occupations.

Mill goes on to make an even stronger claim. It was not only that men have wanted women's subservience, they have wanted them to accept this subservience willingly. Women had been brought up to believe that their ideal character was to be submissive and yielding. They were told it was their duty to live for others, in particular for their husband and children. 'All men, except the most brutish, desire to have, in the women most nearly connected to them, not a forced slave but a willing one; not a slave merely, but a favourite.' What a challenge this sentence must have been to its Victorian readers! It condemns most men and all women who accept their own subordination.

Mill turns to a more positive line of argument. He asserts that it is a characteristic of the modern (Victorian) age that 'human beings are no longer born to their place in life ... but are free to employ their faculties ... the things in which the individual is the person mostly directly interested, never go right but as they are left to his own discretion'. This is, in effect a neat summing up of his argument in *On Liberty*. And why, he now says, should this not be applied to women and girls? By reminding his readers that they have enjoyed a large amount of social progress, Mill hopes that they will see that it is an anomaly to confine women to their traditional role.

Mill next deals with what has always been the first argument for the subjection of women, that men and women are different by *nature*. This word always has to be treated with suspicion. It needs to be defined carefully, because what is considered 'natural' is often only custom or tradition. This is Mill's argument. What the Victorians called the nature of women was, he thought, 'an eminently artificial thing – the result of forced repression in some directions, unnatural stimulation in others'. It had in fact been distorted by the circumstances in which women had lived. It is true that there are physical differences between the sexes, but beyond that, Mill said, we simply do not have enough knowledge about the psychological differences.

Men generally alleged that it was the natural vocation of a woman to be a wife and mother. But if men really believed this, why did they make it so difficult for women to do anything else? Mill argued that in British society of the nineteenth century, because they had no alternatives, women were more or less forced to become wives and mothers. And he made a comparison with the compulsion of slavery or of the press gang for getting sailors into the navy. If women felt forced to marry through lack of alternatives, this suggested that the state of marriage was not especially desirable.

WOMEN AND THE LAW

In the second part of the book, Mill looked at the oppressions of Victorian marriage law and made his own proposals for reform.

If society believed that marriage was the best destination for women, then it ought to make it a more attractive position. However, as things stood, a wife's legal position was very weak: 'she vows a lifelong obedience to him at the altar, and is held to it all through her life by law.' A wife could have no property of her own, which made her position worse than that of a Roman slave, who was allowed a few personal belongings. Both common and statute law sanctioned domestic violence. Rape by a husband of his wife would not be prosecuted, and wife-beating was very rarely prosecuted.

Mill conceded that he was describing the legal position and not the actual treatment of many wives, which was often better than the minimum required by law. Still, was it right to judge an institution by its best examples? No – the laws should be changed to accommodate the bad examples.

Mill also deals with the claim that a family must have a ruler, just as a society must have government. In reply Mill first points out that this 'one-master' argument is untrue, as business partnerships are common and successful. Second, it is easy enough to make arrangements to accommodate the argument. Even if one person should have sole control, this does not have to be the same person. A married couple can divide the responsibilities of a household.

There is a third point that is left open by Mill, but which he does not make explicit. This is that if there has to be one master, it does not have to be the man. He probably felt that to state this in so many words would have been more than his Victorian audience could take.

Mill then argues that men and women should be equal before the law. He proposed legal reforms such as giving married women the right to hold property, equal custodial rights for mothers and fathers, and equal grounds for legal separation. Mill predicts 'an order of things in which justice will again be the primary virtue ... the true virtue of human beings is fitness to live together as equals.'

WOMEN AND WORK

In the third part, Mill argued for women having the vote and that they should be able to take on all of the work that men do. Fortunately, these are both cases where the battle has largely been won. Nevetheless Victorian women were caught in a dilemma. They were not free within marriage and they were not truly free not to marry. An unmarried woman could do little. She could not attend university. If she somehow gained a professional education, the professional associations usually refused to allow her to follow it. Working-class women were handicapped by the very low wages on offer.

The restrictions on women were largely based on beliefs about what they were best fitted to do, so Mill had more dismantling to carry out. In the first part of the book, Mill had declared that there was practically no evidence to show that the differences between men and women were natural and not the result of differences in education and circumstances.

He now takes a different tack by suggesting that, after all and as far as experience shows, women do have characteristic tendencies and aptitudes. For one thing, women seem to have a tendency towards the practical. They have a reputation for 'intuitive perception' which Mill interprets as 'a rapid and correct insight into present fact' and has nothing to do with theory. 'A woman usually sees much more than a man of what is immediately before her.'

To digress for a moment, Mill records the value, for anyone with a speculative mind, of having the counterbalance of 'this lively perception and ever-present sense of objective fact'. For a moment we can see something of the relationship between Mill and his wife, Harriet. He refers to the companionship and criticism 'of a really superior woman. There is nothing comparable to it for keeping his thoughts with the limit of real things, and the actual facts of nature.'

To return to the 'tendencies' of women in general, Mill says they also have a greater quickness of apprehension. What about the allegation of their 'greater nervous susceptibility'? If this were the case, then it might really make women less suited for serious work. Mill declares that this is the result of the way women were brought up. Since so many activities were not allowed to them, they had no outlet for their energy. Besides that, men of a nervous temperament were not excluded from working, so why should women be?

So far, then, the 'difference' argument had nothing to go on. But Mill was still trying, as it were, to find whether there were any grounds for it and so he turned to a question which is still regularly raised in some form or another: why is it that no woman has produced a first-rate work of philosophy, science or art?

Mill offers a number of considerations to explain this. Due to social circumstances only a few women had ever attempted these disciplines. Then there was the point that women had not had the opportunity to acquire the necessary knowledge and training. Also, they were unlikely to have the time, especially if they had a household to run. Nor were women so ambitious for fame and reputation.

In short, Mill gave a social explanation for why women had failed to produce great artistic works. Much the same line was taken about 20 years ago by the feminist writer, Germaine Greer, to explain, in her book, *The Obstacle Race*, why no female artists had achieved the stature of Leonardo, for example, or Michelangelo or Rembrandt.

Since Mill wrote, the fields in which women have failed to produce highly original work have diminished. Jane Austen and George Eliot have produced first-rate works in literature. There have been great female musicians, both vocal and instrumental, and great actresses. Curiously though, the question is still raised about philosophy: why have there been no front-rank female philosophers?

THE BENEFITS OF EQUALITY

In the final part of *The Subjection of Women*, Mill argued for the positive benefits that would come from giving women freedom and equality. It is a largely utilitarian justification, similar to the one he gave in *On Liberty*.

Obviously, women would benefit as individuals from gaining their freedom. But this alone was unlikely to cut any ice with those who supported the overall subservience of women.

The first general benefit, according to Mill, would be the advantage of having 'the most universal and pervading of all human relations regulated by justice instead of injustice'. Second, to give women free use of their faculties and free choice of what they did would be to double the amount of 'mental faculties available for the higher service of mankind'. In effect, there would be an enlargement of the intellectual power available to human beings. Third, women's beneficial influence on society would increase. Because of their physical weakness, women discourage violence and promote the humanizing effects of civilization.

From these considerations, Mill moves to suggesting what true harmony in marriage is: 'two persons of cultivated faculties, identical in opinion and purposes, between whom there exists the best kind of equality, similarity of powers and capacities.'

Throughout the book, one of Mill's underlying arguments was that the subjection of women is a historical relic of primitive social relations. As civilization has progressed, the rule of force has given way before the powers of reason, justice and freedom. Slavery had been done away with, tyrannical government replaced by democratic processes. Yet women, half the human race, had been left behind. 'The moral regeneration of mankind will only really commence, when the most fundamental of the social relations is placed under the rule of equal justice, and when human beings learn to cultivate their strongest sympathy with an equal in rights and cultivation.' Powerful, optimistic words.

However, after all these further considerations, Mill returns to the point he made at the beginning of this fourth part. 'The most direct benefit of all, the unspeakable gain in private happiness to the liberated half of the species; the difference to them between a life of subjection to the will of others, and a life of rational freedom. After the primary necessities of food and raiment, freedom is the first and strongest want of human nature.' This emphasises the themes of *On Liberty* and the importance of freedom to all human beings.

FEMINIST CRITICISMS

Mill's defence of women was extremely controversial for its day. There has been modern controversy about it too, for some feminists have felt that Mill missed opportunities for strengthening the feminist case.

One criticism is that he largely accepted the notion that, once married, a woman should concern herself with the household and her children. It was for the man to provide the family income. Mill is condemned for failing to see that to make women responsible for the home was itself a hindrance to their taking a full part in public life. Furthermore, radical feminists would argue that the household, tended by the wife, and its income provided by the man, must lead to the women's oppression. It does seem rather unfair to criticize Mill, who was so radical for his time, for not being radical enough. But this is a risk that all reformers run. What this criticism amounts to is that it is not possible to have proper equality in marriage where one partner works and the other looks after the household. Mill, I think, might have answered that this is a matter of experience. He would have claimed that these relationships are possible but it would take time and changes in the law to produce more examples. And he certainly thought that he and Harriet had achieved an equal relationship.

Feminists have also been made unhappy by Mill's change of approach in part three of the book, where, despite what he had said earlier about the difficulty of knowing the true nature of women, he does start writing of women's characteristics. He seems to give away too much to those who would judge women as inferior. The differences that Mill mentions look rather like the often made contrast between male logic and feminine intuition. This, in turn, is dangerously close to saying that women have special talents which equip them for a special, separate role, which usually turns out to be an inferior one.

So why does Mill seem to backtrack on the first statement of his views? If these passages are read carefully it can be seen that Mill is showing his intellectual honesty. On the one hand he said, rightly, that there is a lack of knowledge about women's nature. On the other, it is possible that there are specifically female characteristics. If there are, what is the effect of these on the argument? He is determined to stick to the evidence.

As it happens, present-day feminists are themselves divided as to whether there are special female characteristics. There was at one time a tendency to claim that women's minds can and should be just like men's. But more recently, some have preferred to highlight the differences between the sexes.

It is true, however, that *The Subjection of Women* does have omissions. Mill has nothing to say about sex or contraception. Nor did he take a clear line on divorce.

After the publication of the book, Mill remained closely concerned in feminist campaigning for the last few years of his life. At his death, he bequeathed half his estate to the cause of women's education.

* * * SUMMARY * * *

- Mill's feminism was implicit in the arguments of *On Liberty*.

- *The Subjection of Women* was so radical that it was criticized by Mill's former allies.

- The first part of the book tackles the often prejudiced arguments that have been used to justify man's domination.

- The second part discusses marriage law and how to reform it.

- The third argues for giving women freedom to work as they wish.

- The fourth outlines the benefits to society of giving women freedom.

- There is a division among modern feminists about whether Mill was radical enough.

On politics

Mill had a deep interest in politics all his life, an interest shown in much of his journalism and which culminated in his brief spell as a member of parliament. He was both political thinker and politician – an unusual combination. In this chapter we shall look at some of his political ideas as they were summed up in a book published in 1861, *Considerations on Representative Government*. In this book Mill sets out the reasons why he thinks that representative government or democracy is the best form of government – the theory. Then he goes on to describe how such a form of government should be organized – the practice.

THE THEORY

The early chapters of *Considerations* are very instructive on politics and political change. Mill's wide reading in history means that he can give a variety of examples. Although democracy may now be secure in the West, in many countries of the world government is in flux, suffering from dominating heads of state, military governments, *coups d'etat*, and weak institutions. Mill warns against imposing democracy too quickly on countries that are not yet ready for it, and says that forms of government have to be adapted to the people they are for. However, he continually reminds the reader that governments have to be *for* people.

What are the criteria for a good form of government? The most important is perhaps surprising, but certainly plausible: that a government should 'promote the virtue and intelligence of the people themselves'. So, although a form of government must be geared to the level at which the people are at, it must also move them forward by developing their capacities. A second criterion is the extent to which government can 'take advantage of the amount of good qualities which exist and make them instrumental to the right purposes.'

Using these criteria, Mill concludes that democracy is the best form of government. The ideal form would be one where every citizen has a voice and where, at least occasionally, every citizen takes some part in public affairs. The main reason for this is that the intellectual and moral capacities can best be developed by participation in public affairs. Mill emphasizes this educational aspect. He speaks of 'a school of public spirit'. Without such involvement, most of the community will be 'a flock of sheep innocently nibbling the grass side by side'. In short, democracy best promotes the active character that Mill has praised throughout his work.

In developed societies like Victorian Britain, however, it is not really possible for everyone to take much part in public business. They are simply too large. So democracy must work through elected representatives. 'The meaning of representative government is that the whole people, or some numerous portion of them, exercise through deputies periodically elected by themselves, the ultimate controlling power, which, in every constitution, must reside somewhere.'

The next question is, what should these representatives or 'deputies' or, in the British case, members of parliament, do? Mill's idea is that a parliament or national assembly should *deliberate*. It is not itself fit to govern, but instead 'to watch and control the government: to throw the light of publicity on its acts.' It should be 'the nation's Committee of Grievances, and its Congress of Opinions'. A place where every shade of opinion in the country can be expressed is 'one of the most important political institutions that can exist anywhere.' We can see here the full political implications of his arguments for freedom of speech. But Mill would not have been happy with the present House of Commons. Being so much dominated, in the second half of the twentieth century, by two parties, it has not been able to represent 'every shade of opinion'.

The framing of legislation should be left to experts and administration to professional administrators. Parliament would not appoint ministers but rather follow the usual practice by which the Prime

Minister is nominally appointed by the Crown (though in reality by parliament) and chooses his own cabinet. There is one significant difference from the British practice, however. Mill wrote before a system of party politics had developed fully and he was himself opposed to it.

Mill also has a chapter on the dangers of representative government. One which he identifies is apathy, a danger which is of some concern to present-day politicians, since the number of people voting in elections appears to be declining. It may be, however, that this decline is not apathy about politics, but cynicism about politicians. They are seen as self interested and without the public interest at heart – a point Mill was concerned with, as we shall see a little later.

The major risk is one that was mentioned in *On Liberty*, the tyranny of the majority over minorities. It is the danger of government for 'the immediate benefit of the dominant class, to the lasting detriment of the whole.' He gives a specific example of this, the possibility that if the working classes were to receive the vote, they would be powerful enough to vote for legislation that suited them alone. Therefore, in the arrangements for representative government there should be a balance, so that no one class or section of society can dominate.

THE PRACTICE

Mill has argued that it is the job of representative assemblies to represent all opinions. How are they to do this? He suggests a system of proportional representation, which he based on one published a few years before by Thomas Hare. It is a rather complicated scheme. One of its features was that voters did not have to vote for local candidates but could choose from the whole range of candidates throughout the country. So small minorities could put their votes together to elect an MP to their taste. This also seemed to Mill to be a way of getting more talented MPs, because the voters need not be restricted to the 'two or three perhaps rotten oranges, which may be the only choice offered to him in his local market.'

Mill then went on to deal with the question of extending the vote. He wanted an extension because otherwise some citizens would be excluded from having a voice. And he repeats the point made earlier, that political involvement is a kind of education: 'unless substantial mental cultivation in the mass of mankind is to be a mere vision, this is the road by which it must come.'

At the same time, Mill added some restrictions to who should get the vote, which have seemed excessive to modern readers. He said that voters should be literate. They should have the basic educational equipment to profit from the 'school of public spirit'. This meant that universal education would have to come before universal suffrage. This seems extreme, but it is reasonable to claim that political education is essential in a democracy.

Voters should also be taxpayers. And they should not be receiving parish-relief, a nineteenth century equivalent to social security payments. This was on the grounds that if a man could not support himself by his own labour, he should have no claim on public money. This is a very harsh view, for it implies that a man had only himself to blame if he were out of work. Added to this, anyone in this unfortunate position is still expected to obey the laws and might be called upon to fight for his country.

Nonetheless, Mill was less interested in these exclusions than in a more positive proposal. He argues that the votes of the mentally superior should be given more weight. With extension of the vote nearly everyone would be given a voice. But in Mill's opinion the contributions of the intelligent and educated are worth more than that of the ignorant and so they should be given more votes. Mill explains how these tests for intelligence can be carried out and it is some relief for modern readers that having a plural vote does not depend upon social position. However, these pages are uncomfortable reading. In making this argument for plural votes, Mill appears to assume that the intelligent are more likely to think in terms of the public interest and the less intelligent or less well educated, more likely to think only of themselves. This is debatable.

It is more reassuring to find Mill arguing for votes for women, as we would expect. Everything he has said about government and universal **suffrage**, so far in the book, applies to women as well as men. 'I have taken no account of difference of sex. I consider it to be as entirely irrelevant to political rights, as difference in height or in the colour of the hair' is his crisp way of putting it.

KEYWORD

Suffrage: the right or power to vote.

There is one more surprising proposal. Mill was opposed to secret ballots. His basic point was that a person giving his vote had a duty to give it according to his opinion of what was in the public interest. If the ballot was secret, then the voter can use his vote entirely in his own interest. Mill makes a very striking claim. In any political election 'the voter is under an absolute moral obligation to consider the interest of the public, not his private advantage, and give his vote to the best of his judgement, exactly as he would be bound to do if he were the sole voter, and the election depended upon him alone.'

There was no longer any need, Mill thought, for secrecy because of the risk of bribery or intimidation. By doing away with it, voters would find it more difficult to vote for their purely selfish interest. If others knew what they had voted, they could be called to account, in the same way that MPs in parliament, who do not vote secretly, are accountable to their constituents.

Modern readers may make of this what they will. To get us to vote in the public interest rather than self-interest is certainly a worthy aim. Modern politicians who seek our votes seem to appeal a lot to our self-interest.

MILL THE DEMOCRAT

These are the most interesting issues in what is quite a long work. Mill does tackle a number of others, which can only be mentioned briefly here.

Mill has a discussion of whether it is necessary to have a second chamber, such as the House of Lords in Britain, the subject of much discussion at the present time. He thought that if the rest of the constitution is set up correctly, then there is little need for a second chamber. On the other hand, if there is one, it should be able to argue against the first. If the first chamber is an elected body, it represents popular feeling. So the second chamber should have people who are experienced and of proven ability, for example ex-statesmen – but not lords and ladies. Mill thought that the House of Lords (as well as the monarchy) was obsolete. It has taken us over 100 years to catch up with him.

There are chapters too on local government, which Mill would like to see extended because it would involve more people in public affairs, chapters on nationalism, federal governments (as in the USA), and the government of the colonies of empire, in which Mill draws on his experience of the government of India.

To sum up, Mill was a democrat, an assertion largely justified by his desire for universal suffrage, but he appears to be an elitist one. He was writing at a time when there were few democracies in the world and so there was not much experience of what would work and what would not. Calling him a democrat is further justified by the many writings and speeches in which Mill came out in favour of giving a political voice to the working classes. He even supported working-class candidates for parliament with his own money.

Mill was a democrat, but he wanted to oppose the power of the majority and increase the chances of the minority opinion being heard. In the end, the majority must prevail because that is democracy, yet there must be a strong opposition to it for that democracy to be a healthy one.

* * *SUMMARY* * *

- Mill was interested in politics all his life. His views are summarized in his book *Considerations on Representative Government*.

- The best form of government is one that does most to 'promote the virtue and intelligence of the people themselves'.

- Democracy does this best.

- He argued that parliaments and national assemblies should be places where every shade of opinion could be expressed.

- The practical reforms that Mill argued for include proportional representation, plural voting and an end to the secret ballot.

10 The polymath

Mill's writings about morality and politics are read today because it is in those areas that his ideas are most alive. However, he had wider interests than these in philosophy and wider interests than philosophy alone. As Alan Ryan, a British philosopher, has put it, 'he constructed an intellectual system which spanned the horizon from the syllogism to socialism'. Mill valued what he called many-sidedness and he was able to achieve it in his own life.

Mill's *Collected Works* extend to 33 thick tomes. Among them are volumes of essays on:

* Literary topics.

* Economics and society.

* England, Ireland and the Empire.

* Ethics, religion and society.

* Philosophy and the classics.

* Politics.

* French history.

* Equality, law and education.

* India.

In this chapter, we shall take a brief look at the other books that Mill published in his lifetime.

A SYSTEM OF LOGIC

Mill's first important philosophical work, and the one that established his reputation, was *A System of Logic*, published in 1843. It is a massive volume and deals with many philosophical issues. Naturally it has to say a lot about logic, but there is more to it than that. Its subtitle gives some idea of this: 'Being a connected view of the principles of evidence and the methods of scientific investigation'. As well as being Mill's first philosophical book, it is the most comprehensive. The questions he dealt with cost him more time and effort than any of his other writings.

As the title suggests, the book has a systematic treatment of logic as it had developed up to that time. This was the reason for its success and also why it is no longer read. For after Mill's death, there were immense developments in logic, partly led by Bertrand Russell, Mill's godson, which made his logic obsolete.

The book discusses deduction, including mathematics, and induction, which leads Mill into scientific method. His overall aim was to show that 'all knowledge consists in generalizations from experience'. Some had maintained that the mind had independent access to knowledge, through intuition or some 'inner light'. Mill denied this categorically. In this respect he was in the empirical tradition of British philosophy, following thinkers like Locke and **Hume**.

KEY FACT

David Hume (1711–1716): Scottish philosopher in the empiricist tradition of Locke and the most influential British philosopher.

Mill thought that all natural science was based on experience, by which he meant, to be more precise, knowledge acquired through the senses or through experiment, which supported what was perceived by the senses. He then tried to show that the same applied to what were called, in the nineteenth century, the 'moral sciences', that is psychology and sociology, which would now be called the 'social sciences'.

PRINCIPLES OF POLITICAL ECONOMY

This was Mill's second successful textbook, published in 1848. This book too is not much read, because economics has moved on greatly since he wrote it. Moreover, economists are not much interested in the history of their subject. They tend to treat it as a science and concentrate on developing their technical and analytical skill.

The book deals with what we would call economic theory. One of James Mill's closest friends had been the famous economist David Ricardo (1772–1823), who had written in favour of competition and free trade. Mill, like Ricardo, argued that competition promoted efficiency and usually leads to lower prices. Because it is a textbook, it contains a wealth of detailed information and long discussions of practical implications and economic policies. Mill thought that he was improving on his predecessors by showing greater awareness of social and historical factors.

Three of his discussions are worth mentioning. He questioned the need for continuing growth in economies; he discussed how far government should interfere in a competitive market and he considered the conflict between **capitalism** and **socialism**.

It is one of the most widely-accepted beliefs within economics that national wealth should always continue to increase. Mill argued, on the other hand, that once society had reached a certain level of population and of wealth, economics had done its work and should take second place to the improvement of education and individual culture of its citizens. These social benefits were, in the end, more valuable than simply getting richer: 'the best state for human nature is that in which, while no one is poor, no one desires to be richer.'

KEYWORDS

Capitalism: economic system driven by the profit-motive and dependent on the investment of private capital.

Socialism: an economic theory or system that places the means of production of wealth and the distribution of that wealth in the hands of the community.

On the issue of government interference, Mill is in favour of a policy of *laissez-faire*, that is, non-intervention (from the French phrase meaning 'let do'). This coincides with the arguments for individual freedom he gave in *On Liberty*. However, there is one way in which all governments will interfere in an economy, and that is taxation, because all governments need revenue to exist. So, Mill discusses what are fair principles of taxation. Another issue is, how far should governments be involved in economic activity? Mill allows for exceptions to a policy of *laissez-faire* in order to regulate the market so that it operates fairly. This was an important political issue in Britain in the 1980s and 1990s when Conservative governments aimed at freeing markets as much as possible. Companies complain of being hindered by too much 'red tape', but some regulation is needed to prevent them taking advantage of customers.

Mill also gave an even-handed discussion of the pros and cons of socialism and he shows a real concern about the harms that can be caused by capitalism. He even went so far as to wonder whether society might evolve into a form of socialism. By this he did not mean the kind of state-run socialism practised in the former communist countries of Eastern Europe. He was thinking of small-scale co-operatives. This would be 'the nearest approach to social justice, and the most beneficial ordering of industrial affairs for the universal good, which it is possible to foresee.' Because of his utilitarianism, Mill always has in mind the greatest happiness of all the people within a society. He does not approve of individuals simply gaining as much wealth as they can. But, for people to co-operate among themselves, what is needed is the capacity to sacrifice some of their own self-interest. When humankind became more generally capable of this, then it could be possible to move from capitalism to socialism.

Since the collapse of the Soviet Union and its particular brand of socialism, Mill's ideas in this area have become more relevant. He presents a possibly viable alternative to capitalism. He is perhaps also a good example to economists in his concern for social justice, in addition to the narrower considerations of efficiency, growth and wealth creation. For he argued that everyone within a society should share equally in the benefits of economic success.

AN EXAMINATION OF SIR WILLIAM HAMILTON'S PHILOSOPHY

Mill published the works that made him famous in a burst of intellectual energy after Harriet's death. Besides these shorter works, he began a heavy philosophical work with a heavy title, *An Examination of Sir William Hamilton's philosophy*.

Sir William Hamilton (1788–1856) was, apart from Mill, the best-known name in British philosophy in the first half of the nineteenth century. His ideas were opposed to all that Mill stood for. He was what Mill called an 'intuitionist' – as he put it in his *Autobiography*: 'the notion that truths external to the mind may be known by intuition or consciousness, independently of observation and experience is, I am persuaded, in these times, the great intellectual support of false doctrines and bad institutions ... There never was such an instrument devised for consecrating all deep seated prejudices.'

Mill's book about Sir William Hamilton is now hardly read because its original target is now hardly read. This may be because Mill's destructive criticism was so effective. However, it now seems a shame that Mill devoted so much time and effort in attacking such an easy target. The book did create some philosophical controversy for a while, but after Mill's death it faded away.

AUGUSTE COMTE AND POSITIVISM

There was one other late work of philosophy, published in 1865, the same year as the one on Hamilton. Like that work, it is a settling of accounts. But in this case, Mill had had some sympathy with the ideas of Comte and had corresponded with him for a number of years. It seems that Mill felt that because Comte had become well known, now was the time to point out his faults.

Auguste Comte (1798–1857) was a French philosopher and social theorist. He called his philosophy 'positivism'. He had a complex theory of how societies evolve through different stages, which influenced many Victorian intellectuals, such as the novelist George Eliot. He was also something of an empiricist, like Mill, and also, it seemed to Mill, a utilitarian. But in his later works, Comte proposed a religion of humanity, and this is where he began to go drastically wrong. Humanity would be worshipped by a priesthood of philosophers, with hymns, vestments and all the other paraphernalia of organized religion. The world would be broken up into small republics, each run by bankers. Everything an individual did would be closely regulated. The middle class would be removed and society divided into the rich and the poor. The poor would be allowed free lodging, education, and medical assistance, but otherwise they would live on subsistence wages. Men would rule in families; women would not be allowed to earn money or own property. Divorce would be prohibited. In this utopia, progress would be at an end. There would be no place for independent thought. All books, except 100 of Comte's choosing, would be burnt.

The whole thing is ridiculous, but what horrified Mill was its attack on liberty. For him it was a complete system of spiritual and temporal despotism, 'a system by which the yoke of general opinion, wielded by an organized body of spiritual teachers and rulers, would be made supreme over every action, and as far as is in human possibility, every thought, of every member of the community.'

✳ ✳ ✳SUMMARY✳ ✳ ✳

- Mill's 'many-sidedness' can be seen in the range of topics he covered in his journalism.

- The other books he published in his lifetime were: *A System of Logic* (1843), *Principles of Political Economy* (1848), *An Examination of Sir William Hamilton's philosophy* (1865), *Auguste Comte and Positivism* (1865).

11 Mill's value

The value of a philosopher lies in the strength of his or her ideas. Mill's have worn well. They still have life and vigour. They enable us to begin tackling many of the issues in morality and politics that still matter to the present day: What is the good life? What is happiness? How much freedom should we have? What is democracy? What should be the role of women in modern societies? It is still worth arguing with Mill and learning from him.

Mill has been criticized for not being as deeply original as some other figures in the history of philosophy. This may be right, but it is hardly fair to criticize him for it. It is not something that anybody can help. What he could do, he did as well as he could. His dying words to his step-daughter were quoted earlier, 'You know I have done my work'. He did good work in philosophy and also in the world.

One of the things that is attractive about reading Mill is his recurring theme that all individuals, at whatever level of society, could develop themselves. He also thought they *should* develop themselves – for self-development is a way for the individual to work for the common good. This may sound elitist to modern ears, but the alternative would seem to be complacency about the way people are. Mill had a great belief in education, in what it might achieve, and his goal in education was that people should think for themselves. If he is over-optimistic, this is at times the optimism of a good teacher who knows that he can get more from his students by encouragement rather than by discouragement.

A second attractive characteristic of Mill is his openness of mind. In his defence of free speech he referred to the crucial importance of discussion. This openness, and fairness, is ever-present in his work. What gives his books a lot of their freshness is the sense of debate they contain. The reader feels the movement and interplay of ideas. Mill was quite right to claim that he was superior to most of his contemporaries in his 'ability and willingness to learn from everybody'. One of Mill's friends recorded a conversation with him in which he said that 'the great thing was to consider one's opponents as one's allies; as people climbing the hill on the other side.'

Another of Mill's qualities is that, as a writer, he is easy to approach. Once modern readers have got used to his formal Victorian style, they will find it clear and lucid. The books that are still read now were mostly first published in journals of the day, so they were aimed at the general reader.

A fourth quality, which underlines Mill's modern appeal, is that he is a completely secular philosopher, in that he makes no appeal to anything religious or spiritual. Humans, for him, are part of the natural world, and their actions are to be explained by natural science. Standards of good and evil are human standards. There is no beyond.

The book which most shows these qualities is one that has not been discussed so far, although it has been frequently referred to. It is perhaps the most widely read of Mill's books. This is his *Autobiography*. He began writing in 1853 at a time when he had not written his major works and when he feared an early death from tuberculosis. He set down many of his ideas with an urgency that makes for stimulating reading. He completed the book in 1870 and it was published after his death in 1873.

Autobiography is the easiest of his books to read. It is not a confessional autobiography in the twentieth-century style, but a sincere, honest and moving description of his own intellectual and emotional development. What is also interesting is that it brings out how he developed himself, how he achieved the 'internal culture' that he prized. *Autobiography* is a book that celebrates activity and energy of mind.

In one of his early magazine articles, written in 1832, Mill praised the ancient Greeks for seeing wisdom, not as a private luxury, but as a quality essential to success, a practical weapon of daily life available to all: 'the studies of the closet were combined with, and were intended as preparation for, the pursuits of active life ... wisdom was not something to be prattled about, but something to be done.' Mill sought to do this throughout his life. A final illustration of this comes from 1870.

In that year he gave evidence to a Royal Commission on the Contagious Diseases Acts. These acts had empowered the police to take any woman they suspected of being a prostitute and to subject her to a medical examination for venereal disease. This was because venereal disease was rife. For example, in 1868 nearly half of the out-patients of Guy's Hospital in London were venereal cases. Large numbers of sailors in the Royal Navy were affected. The acts were an attempt to stop the spread of the disease by targeting the women who had it. A number of people, including **Florence Nightingale**, felt that the acts were ineffective and unjust, and made enough fuss for a Royal Commission to be established to examine the matter.

KEY FACT

Florence Nightingale (1820–1910): English reformer, famous for her improvements to hospitals and nursing.

Mill was called to give evidence. He pointed out that the disease could only be passed on by a woman through a man. If the aim of the acts was to protect innocent women and children, then the way to do this was to alter the behaviour of the men and not the women. This line of argument, that men using prostitutes were just as much if not more to blame, does not seem to have occurred to the members of the Commission. A few at least found Mill's suggestion completely shocking.

'Am I to understand', asked one, 'you seriously to propose that in this country we should adopt a system of espionage over every man going into a brothel, and that men seen to go into a brothel should be subject all alike to personal examination?' To which Mill's reply was clear and unwavering. 'I am not suggesting espionage, because I do not recommend the Acts at all: but if it is already in practice on women who go to brothels, I think the women should not be singled out to be subject to examination, but the men should be subjected to it also.'

A perfectly reasonable and logical point, but it took 15 years for the acts to be repealed. Yet it does show Mill's sharpness of mind continuing into his old age, along with a willingness to challenge the predjudices of his society, in order to improve the lives of his fellow human beings.

FURTHER READING

Works by Mill

Mill's major works are easily available in paperback.

On Liberty and other essays, Oxford University Press, 1991
   Contains the main works discussed in this book: *On Liberty*,
   *Utilitarianism, Considerations on Representative Government, The
   Subjection of Women*.

Autobiography, Penguin, 1989

Utilitarianism and other essays, Penguin, 1987
   This contains other relevant writings and also a selection of
   Bentham's writing on the subject, plus a very useful introduction
   by Alan Ryan.

Principles of Political Economy, Oxford University Press, 1994
   A selected edition with a good introduction.

Works about Mill

Ryan, Alan, *J.S. Mill*, Routledge, 1974
   This is now out of print, but is the best overall introduction and
   can still be found in libraries.

Scarre, Geoffrey, *Utilitarianism*, Routledge, 1996
   An excellent history and discussion of utilitarian ethics.

Skorupski, John, (ed), *The Cambridge Companion to Mill*, Cambridge
   University Press, 1998
   Covers many aspects of Mill's thought, but is best read after Mill's
   own works.

Stafford, William, *John Stuart Mill*, Macmillan Press, 1988
   The best short guide to Mill.

Thompson, Mel, *Teach Yourself Ethics*, Hodder Headline, 2000
  Not really about Mill, but this has a good introduction to
  utilitarianism for newcomers to ethics.

Wolff, Jonathan, *An Introduction to Political Philosophy*, Oxford
  University Press, 1996
  An excellent introduction to the subject, with a good chapter on
  Mill.

INDEX